A PREDICTIVE LOGISTIC REGRESSION MODEL OF WORLD CONFLICT USING OPEN SOURCE DATA

I. Introduction

General Issue

The value of knowing the future state of the world is priceless. Numerous government agencies and civilian companies produce models to predict the future state of the world. Gaining information about the future gives these organizations a decided advantage in preparation and planning for future events. Models have the potential to offer valuable insights when applied correctly. The renowned statistician and often quoted George Box said "Essentially, all models are wrong, but some are useful" (Box, 1979). No model will ever accurately predict the future, but some models can offer useful insights and give greater clarity to decision makers. This study develops a model that predicts violent conflict in the world using logistic regression and open source data.

Problem Statement

This study develops a suite of models to predict nations that are in a state of violent conflict using a logistic regression model and open source data. These models are used to predict nations in a violent conflict in 2015.

Research Objectives/Questions/Hypotheses

The objectives of this study are to predict future violent conflict in the world and to identify variables that contribute significantly to violent conflict.

1

Research Focus

This study focuses on logistic regression as the modeling method to predict violent conflict. The years analyzed include 2008 through 2013.

Research Questions

How accurately can a Logistic Regression Model predict the state of the world; can it identify nations that will be in a state of "violent conflict" and nations that will not?

Are there key variables from open source data that contribute to a predictive model of nation conflict?

Given a nation is falsely predicted to be in a violent conflict, how likely is it to enter into a violent conflict the following year or within 2-4 years?

Methodology

Logistic regression is used to construct the models. Three different logistic regression model building techniques are introduced and used in this study. The method to construct the dependent variable is discussed as well as methods to build, screen, and test independent variables.

Assumptions/Limitations

This study assumes that there are variables that contribute to a nation being in a violent conflict and can be used as predictors of violent conflict. It also assumes these predictors remain relevant from year to year. The study assumes that the variable data is accurate and collected in a consistent manner and demonstrates causation of the dependent variable and not just correlation. Three of the variables are classification variables; this study assumes they do not change from year to year.

2

The model is limited by data availability, which mandated a two and three year lag on all of the variables. A model built off of previous year data would be superior to the models in this study but would not answer the study problem. It would serve no purpose to develop a model that accurately predicts 2014 when it is already 2014. At the time this study was conducted, in 2014, most of the data sets were complete up through 2012 and sometimes 2013. To predict into the future, in this case 2015, the model has to rely on two and three year old data. "Black Swan" events, such as Al Qaeda detonating a VBIED on the Golden Mosque and spiraling Iraq into a civil war are nearly unpredictable. This study cannot account for "Black Swan" events. The study was limited by availability of the dependent variable. The Heidelberg Institute for Conflict Research was updating their database and was unable to provide data for this study. The data was collected through AFIT analysis of Heidelberg Institute for Conflict Research pdf documents. The models produced in this study do not accurately predict previously stable nations that enter into a violent conflict by choice. These nations' actions do not typically depend on the factors that lead to violent conflict in less stable nations.

Implications

The recommended model from this study could lend insight into nations that are strong candidates for entering into a violent conflict and nations that are strong candidates for exiting a violent conflict. The study will also identify variables that are key contributors to violent conflict. Identifying these variables could give decision makers focus for their efforts to improve stability in a nation.

3

Overview

The study begins with a review of previous. Next, logistic regression is introduced, followed by a description of the dependent and independent variables. Methods to build models are described and then implemented. Sensitivity of the cutoff value that classifies country conflict state is performed. Finally, the study will conclude with analysis of the models, answers to the research questions and conclusions. A list of 2014 and 2015 predictions are presented.

II. Literature Review

The purpose of this chapter is to provide background information for this study. This chapter will discuss relevant research that informs this study, including a CIA task force study, several Center for Army Analysis (CAA) instability studies and various other indices of instability. The single most influential document for this study is the FACT study conducted by Robert Shearer and analysts from the Center for Army Analysis.

Relevant Research

Numerous previous studies predict instability in nations. Researchers in the Central Intelligence Agency's State Failure Task Force investigated several methods to predict political instability using various methods (logistic regression, neural networks, and Markov models)(Shearer, 2010). The CIA task force achieved over 80% accuracy in predicting instability with a logistic regression model using regime type, infant mortality rate, conflict in bordering states, and state discrimination as predictors(Goldstone, 2005). This CIA funded study used global data from 1955 to 2003. The task force categorized and compiled over 200 major political instability events during this time. The dependent variable was an onset of one of these events, which included Revolutionary Wars, Ethnic Wars, Adverse Regime Changes, and Genocides and Politicides. The task force tested hundreds of independent variables, their interactions and rates of change. This study compiles their own data for the dependent variable, making it very difficult to validate the model's accuracy. The CIA study randomly selects nations to validate their model; the claimed 80% accuracy is not a "whole world" accuracy, but a smaller random sample.

The Center for Army Analysis has conducted multiple studies analyzing instability induced conflict. Three CAA studies are significant. These studies include the Political and Economic Risk in Countries and Lands Evaluations (Ahrens, 1997), the Analysis of Complex Threats studies (Bundy and Mathur, 1997 and O'Brien, 2001a), and the Analysis of Complex Threats for Operations and Readiness study (O'Brien, 2001b). The most accurate model from these studies was a possibility theory model that achieved 90% accuracy in predicting conflict five years into the future. Critics suggested this study was difficult to understand and the results were incomprehensible to staff and senior decision makers.

To produce a more "user-friendly" study the CAA initiated the Forecast and Analysis of Complex Threats (FACT) study in 2007. Shearer and Marvin were the FACT study directors and wrote an article in the Military Operations Research journal *Recognizing Patterns of Nation-State Instability that Lead to Conflict* (Marvin, 2010). They built upon the previous studies done at the Center for Army Analysis to accomplish three tasks. First they identify features that capture the instability of a nation, second they forecast the future levels of these features for each nation and third they classified each future state's conflict potential.

Shearer and Marvin intended to predict the future conflict potential of select nation-states in a simple manner. The study used thirteen unclassified data sets categorized into four of the six PMESII categories; Political, Military, Economic and Social. Infrastructure and Information systems were not included in the FACT study.

The variables are shown below along with their unclassified data source. The data set included the years 1993-2003.

- Political
    - Civil liberties – Freedom House
    - Democracy – Polity IV Project
    - Political rights – Freedom House
- Military
    - Conflict history – Heidelberg Institute of Conflict Research
- Economic
    - Male unemployment – World Bank
    - GDP per capita – World Bank
    - Trade openness – World Bank
- Social
    - Adult Male literacy – World Bank
    - Caloric intake – Food and Agriculture Organization of the United Nations
    - Ethnic diversity – CIA World Fact Book
    - Infant mortality – U.S. Bureau of the Census
    - Life expectancy – U.S. Bureau of the Census
    - Religious diversity – CIA World Fact Book

The conflict history data came from the Heidelberg Institute of Conflict Research(Heidelberg Institute for International Conflict Research, 2014). Conflicts were defined as the clashing of interests on national values and issues and were classified according to amount of violence observed. The four categories were Latent Conflict, Crisis, Severe Crisis and War. Shearer states that historically the United States has not intervened in foreign nations until casualties are experienced so the authors combined the four categories into two; Conflict (Severe Crisis and War) and Peace (Latent Conflict and

Crisis)(Shearer, 2010). Different to Sherarer's study, the 2014 HIIK study categorizes the conflicts into six categories instead of four, as outlined in the methodology section of this paper. Shearer's study consisted of two important assumptions:

1) Nations that experienced conflict are similar in that they share common instability features.

2) The distance between the scaled 13 dimension vectors can serve as a reasonable scale for the similarity between two nation-states.

After the data was collected for each nation Shearer used a visual method to test their assumptions by generating 54 three-dimension plots from each of the possible combinations of 1 political, 1 social and 1 economic/military. Points were colored on historical levels of conflict observed; gray for peace and black for conflict. If the variables were significant the team expected the points to be grouped in a cloud by color. Most of the 54 plots did not show distinct color groups; a few did. The initial verification method was unsatisfying so a second method was explored. The Principal Component Analysis (PCA) method reduced the 13 variables into three dimensions that could be visually analyzed. The three components were assigned the terms "social", "political" and "military/economic". The PCA method searches for linear combinations of the original 13 vectors that best express the variance in the data. Using this method the study graphs distinct conflict (black) and peace (gray) clouds and satisfies the two key assumptions. Because the FACT study uses Principal Component analysis it does not show causation between independent variables and violent conflict.

Shearer used a weighted moving average to predict future values and divided their data set into a training set (first 6 years) and a test set (last 5 years). To classify the future

8

data points derived from the weighted moving averages the team used the K-nearest neighbor algorithm and nearest centroid algorithm. The nearest neighbor proved to be more accurate than the centroid algorithm. They used the same portioning of the data to predict (first 5 years) and test (last 6 years) and adjusted the number of neighbors between 3 and 11. With the nearest neighbor algorithm the team used a simple majority of neighbors to classify their predicted nation status. The K-nearest neighbor, with K=7, performed the best with an 87% accuracy. All the other K-nearest neighbors also achieved over 85% accuracy. The predicted nation scores were classified as peace, conflict or uncertain with about 25% classified as uncertain. Without the uncertain classification, the study prediction accuracy for their validation set was 76% This study relied on the data from the same year in which the conflict was determined.

The Center for Army Analysis adopted Shearer's FACT study method which used a weighted average and K-nearest neighbor algorithm. It has comparable accuracies to earlier studies but with predictions further into the future and is easier to understand (Shearer, 2010).

Valuable insight into grouping the nations of the world in explainable groups came from Hans Rosling. Hans Rosling is a renowned statistician, medical doctor and public speaker. He has accumulated numerous accolades with his innovative statistical methods, including being named by Time Magazine as one of the 100 most influential people in 2012(Christakis, 2012). Mr Rosling is a co-founder of the Gapminder foundation which developed the trendalyzer software system (Gapminder, A fact-based worldview). Mr Rosling has become a prominent public speaker using the trendalyzer software. In a 2006 "Ted Talks" lecture Rosling divides the world into the following six categories: (The best stats you've ever seen, 2006)

- Organization for Economic Co-operation and Development (OECD) nations
- Latin America nations
- East European nations
- East Asian nations
- South Asian nations
- African nations

Rosling further subdivides the African nations into Sub Saharan African nations and Arab states (includes much of Middle East). These groupings of nations will inform nation groupings in this study. A list of countries in each group is available in Appendix A.

Directly related to countries in conflict is a country's aptitude to become a failed state. The Fund for Peace provides an index of fragile states in the world (The Fund for Peace , 2015). The fragile states index measures fragile states and ranks them for likelihood of failing. The 2013 fragile state index ranks all countries using 12 variables to determine a final failed state index. These variables include:

- Demographic Pressures
- Refugees and Internally Displaced Persons
- Group Grievance
- Human Flight
- Uneven Development
- Poverty and Economic Decline
- Legitimacy of the State
- Public Service
- Human Rights
- Security Apparatus

- Factionalized Elites
- External Intervention

These 12 variables are significant factors for failed states and are also potential factors for predicting violent conflict. The fragile state list provides a separate index to compare the results of this study with.

Open source data for stability models is available from several reputable sources. The study's independent variables come from four places; the World Bank, CIA World Factbook, Freedom House and the Center for Systemic Peace.

The World Bank was established in 1944, is headquartered in Washington DC and has more than 10,000 employees in more than 120 offices worldwide (World Bank, 2015). This organization has thousands of data sets. The CIA World Factbook provides information on the history, people, government, economy, geography, communications, transportation, military and transnational issues for 267 world entities (Center for Systemic Peace, 2014). Freedom House, established in 1941, is an independent watchdog organization originally created to encourage popular support for American involvement in World War II. In the 1970s Freedom House began to focus on a global view of civil liberties and political rights, publishing its first annual publication "Freedom in the World" in 1973 (Freedom House, 2012). The Freedom House organization provides nation scores for civil liberties and political rights. The Polity IV project is created by the Center for Systemic Peace (CSP) which is a not-for-profit organization that monitors political behavior in each of the world's major states. They record data for 167 nations (Center for Systemic Peace, 2014).

The literature review for this study focused on work performed by Robert Shearer, the Center for Army Analysis, and available data sources. A CIA study provided valuable information on previous logistic regression models and variables that were significant for them. The best CIA model was able to predict with 80% accuracy. Shearer constructed a model that used a K-nearest neighbor algorithm and achieved 76% accuracy over six years.

III. Methodology

Chapter Overview

This chapter discusses the various methods used for this study. The chapter begins with a review of logistic regression; the regression tool used to construct the models in this study. The section on logistic regression includes a summary of logistic regression, a discussion of the logistic regression statistics, and a review of the logistic regression goodness of fit tests. The next section includes the method to select the nations to model followed by a description of the dependent variable. Other discussions include the method to select and screen the independent variables as well as impute missing data. The database used for analysis is discussed as well as a description of the training and test data sets. Three different methods to construct a model are introduced. The chapter finishes with a discussion on methods to analyze only nations that enter into a violent conflict and nations that exit a violent conflict.

Logistic Regression

Before understanding logistic regression it is important to understand why linear regression cannot be applied when dealing with a dichotomous dependent variable. The response for this study is either "in a violent conflict" or "not in a violent conflict", which is dichotomous. Linear regression is the usual method for predicting a response, however, linear regression relies on some primary assumptions, listed below, that are unmet with a dichotomous dependent variable.

1. **Measurement**: All independent variables are interval, ratio, or dichotomous, and the **dependent variable is continuous**, **unbounded**, and measured on an interval or ratio scale
2. Specification. All relevant predictors of the dependent variable are included in the analysis
3. Expected value of error. The expected value of the error is 0, or can be transformed to be so.
4. Linearity: Predictors are linearly related to the Dependent Variable
5. **Homoscedasticity: Residual variance is constant about the regression surface**
6. **Normality: of the distribution residuals**
7. No autocorrelation among error terms
8. No correlation between the error terms and the independent variables
9. Absence of perfect multicollinearity

(Menard, 2001)

When assumptions are violated the model can have serious consequences and lead to wrong conclusions. Transformations are one way to deal with violated assumptions. A number of these assumptions are violated when the dependent variable is dichotomous: Consider the linear equation

$$y_i = x_i'\beta + \varepsilon_i$$

Equation 1: Linear Equation

There are some basic problems with this regression model when using a dichotomous dependent variable. If the response is binary, then the error terms ε_i can only take on two values, 1 and 0. This means the error terms in this model cannot be normal. (Montomgery, 2012) Therefore, the **Normality assumption** is violated. The error variance is not constant, since $\varepsilon_i = y_i - p_i$ and p_i is a constant and y_i takes on the values of either 1 or 0, therefore ε_i changes for each i and the **homoscedasicity** (constant variance) assumption is violated. Not all independent variables for this study are interval, ratio, or dichotomous and the dependent variable is not continuous and it is bounded.

Therefore the **Measurement** assumption is violated. The response is constrained

between 0 and 1. A linear function could include values that lie outside this interval, as

shown in Figure 1. The logistic regression response in this figure is constrained between

0 and 1 over the interval from 0 to 3 while the linear line is not.

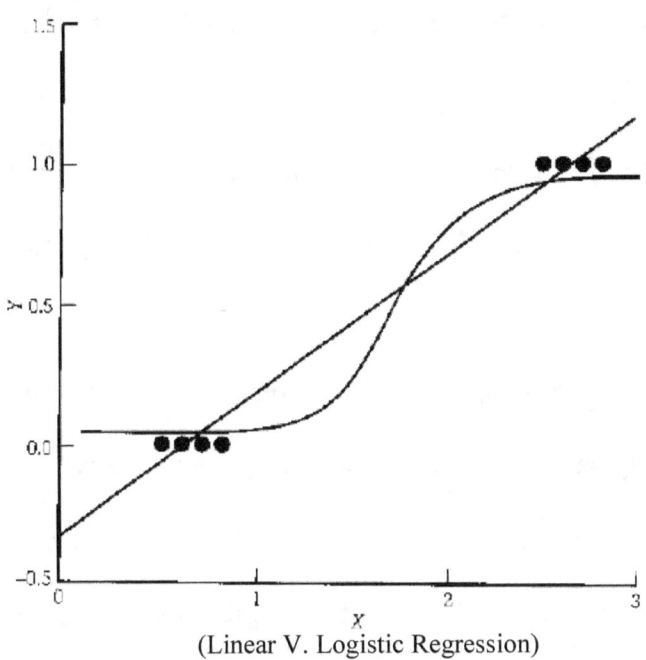

(Linear V. Logistic Regression)

Figure 1: Linear and Logistic Functions

With all the previously stated issues, a linear equation cannot be applied when the

dependent variable is dichotomous. A monotonically increasing (or decreasing) S-

shaped function is usually employed (Montomgery, 2012). An example of this S

shaped function is portrayed in Figure 1, along with a linear function. This nonlinear

function has the form shown in Equation 2 and is called the logistic response

function and has the form.

$$E(y) = p = \frac{e^{x'\beta}}{1+e^{x'\beta}} = \frac{1}{1+e^{-x'\beta}}$$

Equation 2: Logistic Response Function

If we use the natural logarithm of the dependent variable we no longer face the problem that the estimated probability may exceed the maximum or minimum possible values for the probability. The values will be contained between 0 and 1. If a value is less than .5 it will be rounded to 0 (not in a violent conflict), if a value is greater than or equal to .5 it will be rounded to 1 (in a violent conflict). Figure 1 depicts OLS and a logistic regression for the same data points. The OLS line predicts values lying outside of the allowable range (less than 0, greater than 1) while the logistic regression line is bounded by 0 and 1.

Logistic regression is applied when the response variable has only two possible outcomes, generically called success and failure and denoted by 0 and 1 (Montomgery, 2012). The mean response for a success is a probability so the model is written in terms of a probability formula (Myers, 2007). Given regressors x , the logistic response function is shown in Equation 2, where p is the probability of success (Menard, 2001). The probability of failure is 1-p, so that all probabilities sum to 1. The portion $x'\beta$ is called the linear predictor and in the case of a single regressor x may be written as $x'\beta = \beta_0 + \beta_1 x$ (Montomgery, 2012).

Now since the expected value of the error is 0 ($E(\varepsilon_i) = 0$), the expected value of the response variable is $E(y_i) = 1(p_i) + 0(1 - p_i) = p_i$. This implies that $E(y_i) = x'_i\beta = p_i$.

Therefore, the expected response given by the response function $E(y_i) = x_i'\beta$ is simply

the probability that the response variable takes on the value 1.

Logit Transformation

The logistic response function can be made linear. This is called the logit

transformation and is shown in Equation 3.

$$x'\beta = \eta = \ln\frac{p}{1-p}$$

Equation 3: Logit Transformation

The probability, p, and the ratio $\dfrac{p}{1-p}$ in the transformation are called the odds.

The method of maximum likelihood is used to estimate the parameters in the linear

predictor $x'\beta$. Each sample observation follows the Bernoulli distribution, so the

probability distribution of each same observation is

$$f_i(y_i) = p_i^{y_i}(1-p_i)^{1-y_i}, \quad i=1,2,...,n$$

The observations are independent so the likelihood function is:

$$L(y_1, y_2,..., y_n, \beta) = \prod_{i=1}^{n} f_i(y_i) = \prod_{i=1}^{n} p_i^{y_i}(1-p_i)^{1-y_i}$$

Equation 4: Likelihood Function

It is convenient to use the log- likelihood because this value, when multiplied by -

2, is χ^2 distributed.

17

$$\ln L(y_1, y_2, ..., y_n, \beta) = \ln \prod_{i=1}^{n} f_i(y_i) = \sum_{i=1}^{n} [y_i \ln(\frac{p}{1-p})] + \sum_{i=1}^{n} \ln(1-p)$$

Or

$$\ln L(y, \beta) = \sum_{i=1}^{n} y_i x_i' \beta - \sum_{i=1}^{n} \ln(1 + e^{x_i'\beta})$$

Equation 5: Log Likelihood Function

Various software packages use iterative methods to find the maximum likelihood estimator (MLE) by changing the values of β to maximize $\ln L(y, \beta)$.

Odds Ratio

The odds ratio can be interpreted as the estimated increase in the probability of success associated with a one-unit change in the value of the predictor variable (Montomgery, 2012). The odds ratio is designed to determine how the odds of success increases as certain changes in regressor values occur (Myers, 2007). Equation 6 shows an example, if we wanted to determine the odds ratio for a variable decreasing by a value of one.

$$OR = \frac{\text{odds of violent conflict for nation with Variable} = 3}{\text{odds of violent conflict for nation with Variable} = 2}$$

$$= \frac{e^{\beta_0 + \beta_1(3)}}{e^{\beta_0 + \beta_1(2)}} = e^{\beta_1(1)} = 1.5$$

Equation 6: Example Odds Ratio

18

The value of 1.5 is notional but can be interpreted as the odds of violent conflict is enhanced by a factor of 1.5 when the variable is decreased by 1.

Logistic Regression Goodness of Fit Tests

Goodness of fit tests that are used with linear regression do not apply with logistic regression. Other goodness of fit tests are needed.

Likelihood Ratio Test

A likelihood ratio test can be used to compare a "full" model with a "reduced" model. A "reduced" model is a model with just the intercept (β_0) and a "full model" is a model with the intercept and variable(s). The likelihood ratio (LR) test procedure compares twice the logarithm of the value of the likelihood function for the full model (FM) to twice the logarithm of the value of the likelihood function of the reduced model (RM) to obtain a test statistic. Equation 7 shows the LR test statistic.

$$LR = 2\ln\frac{L(FM)}{L(RM)}$$

Equation 7: Likelihood Ratio Test Statistic

The LR test statistic follows a chi-square distribution with degrees of freedom equal to the difference in the number of parameters between the full and reduced models. Therefore, if the test statistic LR exceeds the upper α percentage point of this chi-square distribution, we would reject the claim that the reduced model is appropriate and conclude the additional variable(s) provide a better model (Montomgery, 2012). This

19

hypothesis is the tool used to create logistic regression models for this study. An example of this hypothesis and decision rule is shown below.

Ho: The model containing just the intercept is sufficient
Ha: The model with the additional variable has more explanatory power

The decision rule for this hypothesis is to reject Ho if the -2 log likelihood (-2LL) is greater than the Chi squared statistic with a given alpha and degrees of freedom.

R squared Analogues

The traditional R^2 statistic is not appropriate for logistic regression, however a number of R^2 analogues have been created in order to test a model's goodness of fit.

Likelihood ratio R square (R_L^2)

R_L^2 is a proportional reduction in -2LL or a proportional reduction in the absolute value of the log-likelihood measure, where the -2LL or the absolute value for the log likelihood – the quantity being minimized to select the model parameters is taken as a measure of "variation". Equation 8 shows the equation for the Likelihood ratio R square and Figure 2 shows the conditions for the equation (Menard, 2001).

$$R_L^2 = \frac{G_M}{D_0} = \frac{G_M}{G_M + D_M}$$

Equation 8: Likelihood Ratio R Square

Figure 2: Conditions for the Likelihood Ratio R Square

Un-Adjusted Geometric Mean R Square (R_M^2)

Another R squared analogue, the unadjusted statistic can never have a value of one, which was the motivation for the adjusted geometric mean. Equation 9 shows the equation for the Un-Adjusted Geometric mean R Square and Figure 3 shows the conditions for the equation (Menard, 2001).

$$R_M^2 = 1 - \left(\frac{L_0}{L_M} \right)^{\frac{2}{N}}$$

Equation 9: Un Adjusted Geometric Mean R Square

Figure 3: Conditions for the Un-Adjusted Geometric Mean R Square

Adjusted Geometric Mean R Square (R_N^2)

An adjusted geometric mean square improvement per observation R_N^2 can have a value of 1 by dividing by the maximum possible value of R_N^2 for a particular dependent variable in a particular data set. This is the R squared statistic offered in JMP titled "Generalized R Square". Equation 10 shows the equation for the Adjusted Geometric mean R square and Figure 4 shows the conditions for the equation (Menard, 2001).

$$R_N^2 = \frac{1 - \left(\frac{L_0}{L_M}\right)^{\frac{2}{N}}}{1 - L_0^{\frac{2}{N}}}$$

Equation 10: Adjusted Geometric Mean R Square

Where:
- L_0 is the likelihood function for the model that contains only the intercept
- L_M is the likelihood function that contains all the predictors
- N is the total number of cases

Figure 4: Conditions for the Adjusted Geometric Mean R Square

Hosmer-Lemenshow (HL)

This test groups the observations to perform a goodness of fit test. The observations are classified into groups based on the estimated probabilities of success. Normally, 10 groups are used. An equation for HL is shown in Equation 11 and the conditions for the test are shown in Figure 4 (Montomgery, 2012). The Chi squared distribution is then applied to the HL statistic. An alpha of .05 is typical and the degrees of freedom is the number of groups – 2. Low values suggest poor goodness of fit and the model is rejected.(Allison, 2013)

$$HL = \sum_{j=1}^{n} \frac{(O_j - N_j \bar{\pi}_j)^2}{N_j \bar{\pi}_j (1 - \bar{\pi}_j)}$$

Equation 11: Hosmer Lemenshow

> **Where:**
> • O_j is the observed number of success
> • $\bar{\pi}_j$ is the probabilty of success for j
> • N_j is the number in the group j

Figure 5: Conditions for Hosmer Lemenshow

There are multiple methods to classify a model and present its accuracy. The overall goodness of a model can be measured by its accuracy. Two such methods are presented here.

Predictive Efficiency

A few tools help demonstrate how well the models predicts. The predictive efficiency statistic, shown in Equation 12, is one such tool.

$$\text{predictive efficiency} = \frac{(\text{errors without model}) - (\text{errors with the model})}{(\text{errors without model})}$$

Equation 12: Predictive Efficiency

23

Confusion Matrix

A second tool to assess model predictability is a confusion matrix. A confusion matrix depicts the number of true negatives, false negatives, false positives and true positives and gives prediction accuracy, shown in Figure 6. (Menard, 2001)

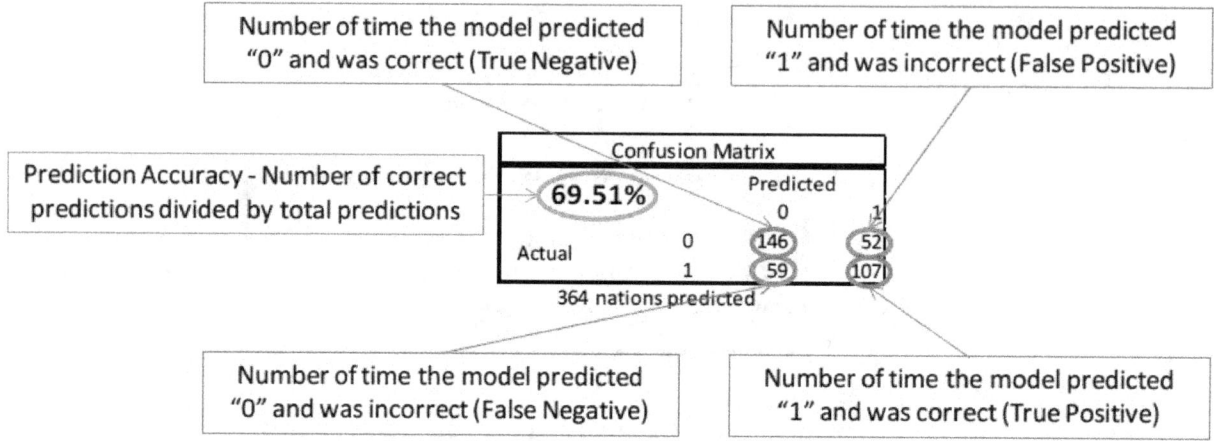

Figure 6: Confusion Matrix

The logistic regression and goodness of fit statistics mentioned above can be computed using computer software. Various software packages can analyze logistic regression with different strengths and weaknesses for each package. This study relies on JMP software because it is user-friendly and sufficiently powerful for this level of analysis.

JMP Software outputs

Many of the statistics discussed are shown below as JMP output. Figure 7 shows example JMP results for a Likelihood Ratio Test, explained previously.

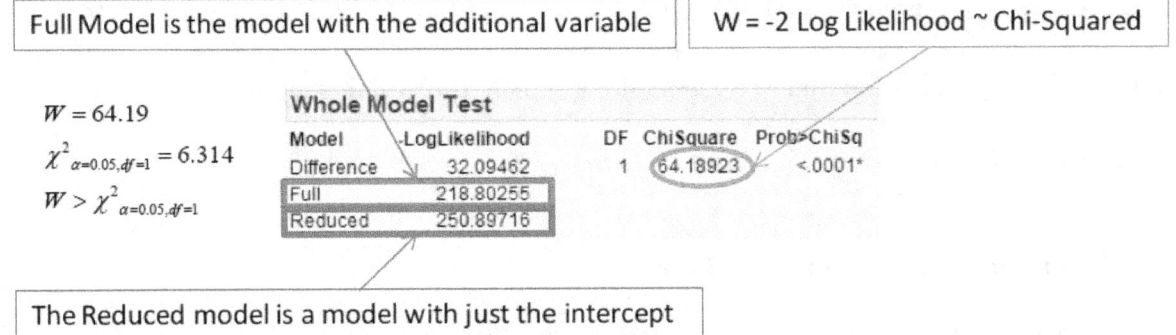

Figure 7: Logistic Regression Test for Significance

In Figure 7, Freedom was the additional variable that was tested for significance. Since W is greater than the Chi Square statistic, the baseline model with just the intercept is rejected, leading to the conclusion the model with the variable "Freedom" has greater explanatory power.

JMP software also offers the Effect Likelihood Ratio Test for each individual variable. An example screenshot is shown in Figure 8.

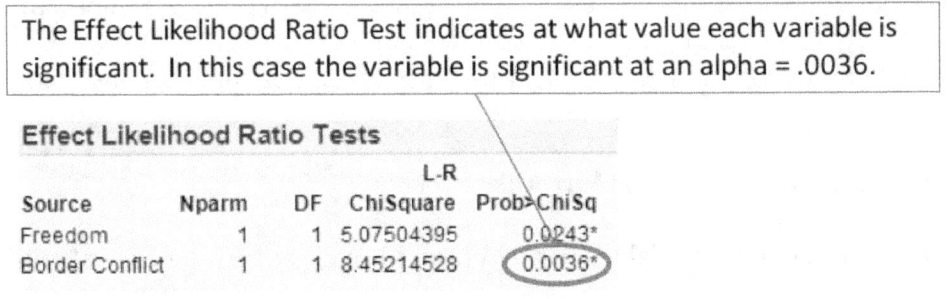

Figure 8: Effect Likelihood Ratio Test

The value in Figure 8, circled in blue, is the difference in the Likelihood Ratio test value of the model with the variable "Border Conflict" in the model compared to without the variable. This statistic can be used to assess the significance of each individual variable in the model. The smaller the value, the more significant the variable. In the

25

example in Figure 8 the variable "Border Conflict" is significant at an alpha = .0036 level. This level is compared to a threshold, a typical threshold is alpha = .05; therefore this variable is considered significant.

Method to Select the nations to Model

This study includes for consideration 180 of the 193 United Nations member nations (United Nations, 2014). It does not include small nations with insufficient data, such as Nauru, Saint Kitts and Nevis, Saint Lucia and Saint Vincent, the Grenadines, Andorra, Monaco, Marshall Islands, Tuvalu, Dominica, Palau, Liechtenstein and San Marino. Disputed states of Abkhazia, Nagorno-Karabakh, Northern Cyprus, Sahrawi Arab Democratic Republic, Somaliland, South Ossetia, Taiwan, and Transnistria are also not included. Added to the United Nations list are Palestine (West Bank and Gaza) and Kosovo. The total number of modeled nations is 182. Not all of these nations have complete data; this problem is addressed later in this study, in the data imputation section. Incomplete data is a common problem, particularly when dealing with unstable nations.

Method to Select the Dependent Variable

This study will use variables derived from "Level's of Violence" calculated by the Heidelberg Institute for International Conflict Research (HIIK) as the dependent variable. The HIIK level of violence is binomial; a nation is either in a violent conflict or it is not for a given year. These two "Levels of Violence" are mapped from six conflict intensity levels which are discussed later. The HIIK publishes conflict data each year, starting in 1992. In 2013 HIIK looked at 414 observed conflicts and required 152 researchers to compile the data (Heidelberg Institute for International Conflict Research,

2014). HIIK data for years 2008-2013 is considered. HIIK uses conflict measures and conflict items to determine political conflict; this study uses the HIIK definitions for these terms as well. Definitions for political conflict, conflict measures and conflict items are provided below.

Political Conflict

*A political conflict is a positional difference, regarding values relevant to a society – the **conflict items** – between at least two decisive and directly involved actors, which is being carried out using observable and interrelated **conflict measures** that lie outside established regulatory procedures and threaten core state functions, the international order or hold out the prospect to do so.* (Heidelberg Institute for International Conflict Research, 2014).

Conflict Measures

Conflict measures are actions and communications carried out by a conflict actor in the context of a political conflict. They are constitutive for an identifiable conflict if they lie outside established procedures of conflict regulations and – possibly in conjunctions with other conflict measures – if they threaten the international order or core function of the state. (Heidelberg Institute for International Conflict Research, 2014).

Conflict Items

Conflict items are material or immaterial goods pursued by conflict actors via conflict measures (Heidelberg Institute for International Conflict Research, 2014).

The HIIK study includes ten different conflict items shown in Table 1.

Table 1: HIIK Conflict Items
(Heidelberg Institute for International Conflict Research, 2014)

The Heidelberg Institute for International Conflict Research Conflict Items	
Item	**Description**
System/Ideology	Conflict actor aspires a change of the ideological, religious, socioeconomic or judicial orientation of the political system or changing the regime type itself
National power	The power to govern a state
Autonomy	Attaining or extending political self-rule of a population within a state or of a dependent territory without striving for independence
Secession	Aspired separation of a part of a territory or a state aiming to establish a new state or to merge with another state
Decolonization	Desired independence of a dependent territory
Subnational Predominance	Attainment of the de-facto control by a government, a non-state organization or a population over a territory or a population.
Resources	Pursued possession of a natural resources or raw materials, or the profits gained thereof
Territory	Desired change of the course of an international border
International Power	Desired change aspired in the power constellation in the international system or a regional system therein
Other	Residual category

Conflict Intensity Level

The six intensity levels presented by the institute have been aggregated into two levels; "Not violent conflicts" and "Violent conflicts" as shown in Table 2. HIIK includes in their analysis 260 countries, islands and territories; some countries have several conflicts. A total of 414 conflicts are scored in 2013. For this study a country will get the highest score for any conflict in which it is engaged.

Table 2: HIIK Intensity Level and Level of Violence

Intensity Level	Terminology	Level of Violence
0	No conflict	Not violenct conflicts
1	Dispute	
2	Non-violent crisis	
3	Violent crisis	Violent conflicts
4	Limited war	
5	War	

To assess the intensity levels of the violent conflicts HIIK measures five proxies; weapons, personnel, casualties, refugees and Internally Displaced Persons (IDPs) and destruction (Heidelberg Institute for International Conflict Research, 2014). These proxies are measured and scored for every region and every month. Table 3 shows the scoring method used by HIIK.

Table 3: HIIK Intensity Level Scoring Method

Personnel

Low	Medium	High
≤ 50	> 50 ≤ 400	> 400
0 point	1 point	2 points

Destruction

Low	Medium	High
Within 0 dimensions	Within 1-2 dimensions	Within 3-4 dimensions
0 point	1 point	2 points

Weapons

		Weapons employment	
		Light	Heavy
Weapon Type	Light		
	Heavy	1 point	2 points

Casualties

Low	Medium	High
≤ 20	> 20 ≤ 60	> 60
0 point	1 point	2 points

Refugees and IPDs

Low	Medium	High
≤ 1000	≥ 1000 ≤ 20000	> 2000
0 point	1 point	2 points

Method to select and screen independent variables and to impute missing data

Twenty-two country statistic variables and four trend variables are considered in the initial analysis. Ten variables are considered from the CAA FACT study and three variables are considered from the CIA study. The study sponsor believed population migrations influenced violent conflict so refugee population seeking asylum and refugee population of origin are both considered. Eight additional variables (Population density, population growth, rural population percent, arable land, birth rate, death rate and fertility rate) were deemed worthy of exploration by the study lead and are also considered in the study. Second order polynomials are introduced later. The four trend variables were included because of their potential to identify trends in a nation that could lead to violence. One additional variable, "Region", is introduced later to explain the regional differences in the world; this variable proves key to the study.

Many of the 2013 data sets are not complete; this will require a two or three year lag in the model in order to predict 2015 nation states. Since this is 2014, predicting 2015 and beyond is the goal of this study. To predict 2015, the model will have to use 2012 and 2013 data. The 26 variables are listed in Table 4. Also listed in Table 4 are the year the dataset was first collected, the data lag and the number of nation entries for 2011-2013 for each variable. Fifteen of the country statistic data sets are from the World Bank; four are from the CIA world Fact book, one from Freedom House, one from the Center for Systemic Peace and one from and the Food and Agriculture organization of the United Nations. Eleven of the independent variables require a 2 year lag and use 2012 data to model 2015, 12 variables require a 3 year lag and 3 variables are locked and do not change. Yearly data is not available for "Regime Type", "Ethnic Diversity" and "Religious Diversity" so these variables do not change from year to year and are considered locked.

Table 4: Country Statistic Variables

Year of first dataset	Lag (yrs)	Variables	Number of entries per year		
			2011	2012	2013
		World Bank variables			
1970	2	Population density (people per sq. km of land area)	181	181	180
1970	2	Population growth (annual %)	181	181	182
1970	2	Rural population (% of total population)	181	181	181
1970	3	Arable land (hectares per person)	181	181	
1970	3	Birth rate, crude (per 1,000 people)	182	182	
1970	3	Death rate, crude (per 1,000 people)	182	182	
1970	3	Fertility rate, total (births per woman)	182	182	
1990	3	Refugee population by country or territory of asylum (percent of pop)	160	159	
1990	3	Refugee population by country or territory of origin (percent of pop)	180	280	
1970	2	GDP/capita (current US$)	178	177	165
1970	3	Mortality rate, infant (per 1,000 live births)	182	182	
1990	3	Improved water source (% of population with access)	174	172	
1991	3	Unemployment, male (% of male labor force) (modeled ILO estimate)	171	171	
1970	3	Life expectancy at birth, total (years)	182	182	
1970	3	Trade (% of GDP)	167	146	92
		CIA World Fact Book variables			
2010	2	Conflict in Bordering States	182	182	182
	Locked	Regime type	182	182	182
	Locked	Ethnic diversity (Percent of dominant ethnic group)	180	180	180
	Locked	Religious diversity (Percent of dominant ethnic group)	178	178	178
		Other			
1973	2	Freedom (Average of Civil Liberties and Political Rights (scores 1 to 7))	180	179	180
1946	2	Polity IV (Political behavior monitor (scores 1 to 10)	158	158	157
2001	3	Caloric Intake (Average caloric intake per person)	165	165	
		Trend Variables			
2011	2	2 yr HIIK intensity level trend	182	182	182
1976	2	2 yr Freedom trend	180	180	180
1977	2	3 yr Freedom trend	180	180	180
1979	2	5 yr Freedom trend	180	180	180

Most of the variables defined above have simple definitions but some of them require additional discussion. Following are expanded descriptions for these variables.

Trade (% of GDP) – This variable is the summation of two other World Bank statistics; Imports of goods and services (% of GDP) and Exports of goods and services (% of GDP)

Conflict in Bordering States – The CIA study cited Border Conflict as one of their significant variables. In this study, "border conflict" accounts for conflict in neighboring states and mimics a "bad neighbor" indicator. The CIA world Factbook publishes the shared land boundaries for each country. This variable will use the following formula to calculate a Border Conflict value for each nation. The formula and an example conflict score are shown in Table 5.

Table 5: Conflict in Bordering States Calculation

$$Cb = \sum_{1}^{n} x_i p_i \qquad \text{where}$$

$Cb =$ Conflict in border states statistic
$n =$ number of bordering nations
$x_i =$ previous year intensity level for nation i
$p_i =$ percent of border shared with nation i

Guatemala example			
	km shared	% of border	2013 Intensity Level
Mexico	958	57%	5
Belize	266	16%	3
El Salvador	199	12%	1
Honduras	244	15%	3
TOTAL	1667		

Guatemala conflict in border states statistic	3.9

$$Cb = .57(5) + .16(3) + .12(1) + .15(3) = 3.9$$

This variable will include a 2 year lag; a model for 2015 will include data from 2013. Twenty nine island nations that have no borders were imputed using JMP software.

Regime type – Regime type is cited by the CIA study as significant. The idea that different types of governments have different propensities for violent conflict necessitates the need for this variable. The CIA World Factbook gives 57 different government descriptions for the 182 modeled nations. These 57 government types were initially mapped to 10 regime types. The variable "Regime type" was quickly removed from trial models because 10 nominative levels proved too many for a dataset that initially only included 114 nations. The old "Regime type" variable was partly responsible for overfitting the initial trial model. In order to include a "Regime type" variable in the model a "New Regime Type" variable was mapped from the original data, including only 3 types of regimes; "Central ruler/ ruling party", "Democratic" and "Emerging, transitional, recent change and disputed". The old Regime variable and new Regime variable are shown in Table 6. For purposes of determing correlations and for factor analysis the regime types were mapped to numbers (Democratic = 1, Central ruler/ruling party = 2, Emerging, transitional, recent change, disputed = 3). In order to allow ordinal mapping of regime categories to a number the study assumes that democratic regimes are preferred to Central/ruling party regimes and both are preferred to Emerging, transitional, recent change, disputed regimes with regard to a nation being in a state of "Not in conflict". This assumption is supported by the corrleation between this mapped set and the dependent variable, shown later. The Freedom equation is shown in Equation 13.

Table 6: Regime Type

Expanded Regime Type	
Class	**Total**
Communist	4
Democracy	39
Dictatorship	2
Military Junta	1
Monarchy	24
Republic	107
Theocracy	2
Transitional Government	2
Disputed	1
Grand Total	**182**

Reduced Regime Type	
New Class	**Total**
Central ruler/ruling party	36
Democratic	137
Emerging, transitional, recent change, disputed	9
Grand Total	**182**

Civil liberties – Civil liberties is the allowance of freedom of expression and belief associational and organizational rights, rule of law, and personal autonomy without interference from the state. Civil Liberties is rated on a scale from 1 to 7; a score of "1" is best.

Political rights – Political rights is also rated on a scale from 1 to 7, it scores the ability of people to participate freely in the political process, including the right to vote, join political parties and elect representatives. A score of "1" is best.

Freedom – Civil Liberties and Political Rights are highly correlated. The Freedom statistic averages the two scores for the country, aggregating the correlated variables into one variable. This is the variable used in this study, not civil liberties or political rights. The FACT studies use both Political Rights and Civil Liberties as variables and the CIA study uses a variable name "State Discrimination". The Freedom variable is introduced in this study to account for a nation's political climate and political oppression. This

34

variable proves to be one of the study's most important variables. The equation for

Freedom is shown in Equation 13.

$$\text{Freedom score} = \frac{\text{Civil Liberty score} + \text{Political Rights score}}{2}$$

Equation 13: Freedom Score

Polity IV – Polity IV Project records individual regime trends from 1946 to 2013. The

Polity IV project is created by the Center for Systemic Peace (CSP) which is a not-for-

profit organization that monitors political behavior in each of the world's major states

(Center for Systemic Peace, 2014). They record data for 167 Nation states. Each nation

is scored between 0 and 10; 10 is the best. When a country is in a state of interruption,

interregnum or transition the score was -66, -77 or -88. These scores were placeholders

to identify nations that cannot be scored and cannot be used in the database. These data

points were deleted, leaving only 157 nations for this variable. The missing data was

later imputed using JMP software, discussed later.

Caloric intake – The Food and Agriculture Organization of the United Nations collects a

myriad of food and agricultural data (United Nations, 2013). One of their metrics

measures the food supply of a country in Kilocalories per capita per day. This data is

collected for years 2001 to 2011. 2011 data is used as a proxy for 2012 data to avoid

using a 4 year lag throughout the model. All of the other variable datasets are complete

through either 2012 or 2013 while Caloric intake only had data up to 2011.

2 yr HIIK intensity level trend - The 2 yr HIIK intensity level trend is calculated with the formula in Table 7. The intensity level, instead of the level of violence (see Table 2) is used to calculate this variable.

Table 7: 2 yr HIIK Trend Formula and Example

$$2013 \text{ HIIK Trend} = \frac{\text{Intensity Level change from 2010 to 2011}}{6 \text{ possible HIIK intensity levels}}$$

Example

$$\text{Belarus Trend} = \frac{3-2}{6} = \frac{1}{6}$$

HIIK Trend Variable (example nations)			
Nation	2010 HIIK Intensity Level	2011 HIIK Intensity Level	2013 HIIK Trend Var
Belarus	2	3	0.167
Belgium	1	1	0
Belize	1	1	0
Benin	0	0	0
Bhutan	2	1	-0.167
Bolivia	3	1	-0.333
Bosnia and Herzegovina	3	3	0
Botswana	2	1	-0.167
Brazil	1	3	0.333

The most current year for HIIK data is 2013. In order to predict conflict in 2015 the HIIK trend variable will look at the trend from 2012-2013 and have a 2 year lag.

Freedom trends – Freedom proved the most significant variable in many models in this study. Three Freedom trend variables are analyzed, 2 yr trend, 3 yr trend and 5 year trend. These variables will require a 2 year lag. Formulas for the three Freedom trends are shown in Equation 14.

$$\text{Year X Freedom 2 yr Trend} = \frac{\text{Score change from (Year X-3) to (Year X-2)}}{7}$$

$$\text{Year X Freedom 3 yr Trend} = \frac{\text{Score change from (Year X-4) to (Year X-2)}}{7}$$

$$\text{Year X Freedom 5 yr Trend} = \frac{\text{Score change from (Year X-6) to (Year X-2)}}{7}$$

Equation 14: Freedom Trend calculations

Screening variables

Variable screening is used to remove some of the variables before initial model building. Multicollinearity, or near-linear dependence among the variables will cause problems in the model. High multicollinearity tends to produce unreasonably high logistic regression coefficients and can result in coefficients that are not statistically significant (Menard, 2001). Variance Inflation Factors (VIFs) are important multicollinearity diagnostics (Menard, 2001). The equation for VIFs is shown in Equation 15.

$$VIF_j = \frac{1}{1 - R_j^2}$$

Equation 15: VIF Calculation

> **Where:**
> R_j^2 is the coefficient of multiple determination obtained from regressing x_j on other regressor variables.

VIFs larger than 10 imply serious problems with multicollinearity (Montomgery, 2012). According to Montgomery, VIFs that exceed 5 or 10 indicate that the associated regression coefficients are poorly estimated. This study uses a VIF value of 10 as a threshold to remove variables. VIFs for all 26 initial variables are shown in the right column of Table 8. The values are calculated with JMP software using a database from 2011 to 2013. Five (boxed in red) variables have VIFs greater than 10.

Table 8: VIF Values for 26 Variables

Parameter Estimates

Term	Estimate	Std Error	t Ratio	Prob>|t|	VIF
Intercept	-3.302587	3.499569	-0.94	0.3460	
HIIK Trend	0.0685622	0.562698	0.12	0.9031	1.0457229
2 Yr Freedom Trend	-0.823791	2.757223	-0.30	0.7653	1.8209053
3 Yr Freedom Trend	-2.456985	2.443008	-1.01	0.3153	3.0813272
5 yr Freedom Trend	1.9793009	2.061165	0.96	0.3376	3.0251145
Pop density	0.0009139	0.00058	1.57	0.1163	1.6429437
Pop growth	0.3846109	0.162218	2.37	0.0183*	9.0964196
Rural Pop	-0.001601	0.005184	-0.31	0.7577	2.8866039
Arable land	0.2226266	0.329614	0.68	0.4999	1.4517194
Birth Rate	0.0530441	0.074191	0.71	0.4752	180.46745
Death Rate	0.039078	0.05928	0.66	0.5102	10.138755
Fertility Rate	-0.620282	0.443711	-1.40	0.1631	118.40483
Refugees Asylum	-0.100238	1.843168	-0.05	0.9567	1.2782438
Refugees Origin	19.046714	10.94383	1.74	0.0828	1.1871471
GDP per Capita	-1.411e-5	0.000007	-2.02	0.0445*	3.4657826
Infant Mortality	0.0078813	0.008487	0.93	0.3538	13.632381
Improved Water	-0.010624	0.010633	-1.00	0.3185	6.3381878
Unemployment	0.0115862	0.013448	0.86	0.3896	1.5941582
Life Expectancy	0.0636347	0.034864	1.83	0.0689	29.868838
Trade	-0.011338	0.002135	-5.31	<.0001*	1.3120713
Caloric intake	0.0000536	0.000244	0.22	0.8264	1.7672086
Freedom	0.4644866	0.091231	5.09	<.0001*	6.9272612
Polity IV	0.1261223	0.045407	2.78	0.0058*	6.682891
Regime Type[Central ruler/ruling party]	-0.339556	0.291673	-1.16	0.2452	3.2685289
Regime Type[Democratic]	-0.336435	0.283272	-1.19	0.2359	3.3956048
Ethnic Diversity	-0.001286	0.003415	-0.38	0.7067	1.6927132
Religious Diversity	0.467412	0.302979	1.54	0.1239	1.3733484
Border Conflict	0.0876431	0.086702	1.01	0.3129	1.9220361

These 5 variables have VIF values greater than 10.

Variables that violate a VIF threshold of 10 are eliminated one at a time. The variable with the highest VIF (Birth Rate) is removed and new VIF values are calculated. This process is continued until all variables have VIF scores less than 10. Using this process, three variables are removed (Birth Rate, Life Expectancy and Fertility Rate). The final VIF values for the remaining 23 variables are shown in Table 9.

Table 9: VIF Values for 23 Variables

Parameter Estimates					
Term	Estimate	Std Error	t Ratio	Prob>|t|	VIF
Intercept	1.571538	1.284418	1.22	0.2220	.
HIIK Trend	0.0446503	0.567585	0.08	0.9373	1.0454044
2 Yr Freedom Trend	-0.835378	2.775577	-0.30	0.7636	1.8130369
3 Yr Freedom Trend	-2.626304	2.459911	-1.07	0.2865	3.0696094
5 yr Freedom Trend	1.8800524	2.044958	0.92	0.3586	2.92578
Pop density	0.0010501	0.000578	1.82	0.0700	1.5993731
Pop growth	0.0636454	0.10829	0.59	0.5571	3.98298
Rural Pop	-0.004746	0.005088	-0.93	0.3516	2.7324355
Arable land	0.1770687	0.330198	0.54	0.5922	1.4314532
Death Rate	-0.061618	0.03481	-1.77	0.0777	3.4350348
Refugees Asylum	-0.687363	1.813726	-0.38	0.7050	1.2161409
Refugees Origin	21.182609	10.8507	1.95	0.0518	1.1466684
GDP per Capita	-8.272e-6	6.259e-6	-1.32	0.1872	2.7283366
Infant Mortality	-0.002923	0.007121	-0.41	0.6817	9.4293789
Improved Water	-0.005981	0.01026	-0.58	0.5604	5.7987981
Unemployment	0.0073985	0.013024	0.57	0.5704	1.4690273
Trade	-0.010424	0.002102	-4.96	<.0001*	1.2497017
Caloric intake	5.8842e-5	0.000245	0.24	0.8103	1.7470231
Freedom	0.4779762	0.090862	5.26	<.0001*	6.7514647
Polity IV	0.1356123	0.045508	2.98	0.0031*	6.5957859
Regime Type[Central ruler/ruling party]	-0.356699	0.290342	-1.23	0.2201	3.1822648
Regime Type[Democratic]	-0.38667	0.284677	-1.36	0.1753	3.3695469
Ethnic Diversity	-0.000814	0.003333	-0.24	0.8071	1.583976
Religious Diversity	0.5092652	0.301274	1.69	0.0919	1.3342517
Border Conflict	0.1148775	0.086896	1.32	0.1871	1.8969373

Removing the three variables reduces the correlations between the variables.

Table 10 and Table 11 shows a heat map of the variable correlations before and after

removing Birth Rate, Life Expectancy and Fertility Rate. There are substantially more

high correlations in Table 10 than in Table 11. Regime type is a nominal data set and is

not included in the tables. Although some high correlations still exist in the remaining

variables, none of the VIF values are greater than 10. Some of the most correlated

variables included the Freedom trend variables with each other, "Infant Mortality" with

"Improved water" and "Freedom" with "Polity IV". This is not surprising, as access to

improved water decreases then infant mortality will naturally increase and the Freedom

Score and Polity IV score are both scores of a nation's political oppressiveness.

Table 10: Correlation Heat Map before Removing Variables

	HIIK Trend	2 Yr Freedom Trend	3 Yr Freedom Trend	5 yr Freedom Trend	Pop density	Pop growth	Rural Pop	Arable land	Birth Rate	Death Rate	Fertility Rate	Refugees Asylum	Refugees Origin	GDP per Capita	Infant Mortality	Improved Water	Unemployment	Life Expectancy	Trade	Caloric intake	Freedom	Polity IV	Ethnic Diversity	Religious Diversity	Border Conflict
HIIK Trend		-0.04	0.00	0.00	-0.01	0.07	0.00	-0.04	0.04	-0.08	0.03	0.05	-0.03	-0.05	0.02	-0.05	-0.02	-0.01	0.02	0.05	0.12	-0.13	0	0.00	0.12
2 Yr Freedom Trend	-0.04	1	0.71	0.55	-0.05	0.07	-0.03	-0.02	0.06	-0.01	0.06	0.05	0.00	-0.01	0.04	-0.07	0.01	-0.04	-0.03	-0.01	0.09	-0.11	-0.03	0	0.03
3 Yr Freedom Trend	0.00	0.71	1	0.78	-0.07	0.10	-0.03	-0.01	0.12	0.02	0.12	0.09	-0.03	-0.02	0.08	-0.15	0.05	-0.08	-0.03	-0.04	0.13	-0.12	-0.05	-0.01	0
5 yr Freedom Trend	0.00	0.55	0.78	1	-0.11	0.13	-0.03	0.01	0.18	0.06	0.20	0.16	-0.05	-0.03	0.12	-0.25	0.11	-0.13	-0.04	-0.07	0.15	-0.13	-0.06	0.02	0.02
Pop density	-0.01	-0.05	-0.07	-0.11	1	0.04	-0.05	-0.17	-0.15	-0.16	-0.14	0.04	-0.04	0.16	-0.13	0.13	-0.09	0.16	0.52	0.20	-0.01	-0.06	0.01	-0.08	0.05
Pop growth	0.07	0.07	0.10	0.13	0.04	1	0.13	-0.15	0.54	-0.18	0.53	0.08	0.09	0.00	0.39	-0.37	-0.20	-0.35	-0.02	0.18	0.42	-0.47	-0.36	0.00	0.30
Rural Pop	0.00	-0.03	-0.03	-0.03	-0.05	0.13	1	-0.11	0.60	0.27	0.57	-0.12	0.16	-0.59	0.59	-0.60	-0.01	-0.63	-0.11	0.28	0.33	-0.30	-0.15	-0.19	0.24
Arable land	-0.04	-0.02	-0.01	0.01	-0.17	-0.15	-0.11	1	-0.05	0.27	-0.03	-0.11	-0.04	0.07	-0.03	0.02	0.02	-0.01	-0.16	-0.23	-0.07	0.08	0.04	-0.08	-0.10
Birth Rate	0.04	0.06	0.12	0.18	-0.15	0.54	0.60	-0.05	1	0.30	0.98	0.08	0.19	-0.53	0.87	-0.81	-0.05	-0.85	-0.24	0.16	0.48	-0.43	-0.36	-0.11	0.30
Death Rate	-0.08	-0.01	0.02	0.06	-0.16	-0.18	0.27	0.27	0.30	1	0.35	-0.17	0.05	-0.18	0.53	-0.34	0.16	-0.62	-0.09	-0.23	0.00	0.09	-0.09	-0.27	-0.26
Fertility Rate	0.03	0.06	0.12	0.20	-0.14	0.53	0.57	-0.03	0.98	0.35	1	0.07	0.21	-0.46	0.85	-0.81	-0.06	-0.82	-0.25	0.12	0.43	-0.39	-0.36	-0.14	0.25
Refugees Asylum	0.05	0.05	0.09	0.16	0.04	0.08	-0.12	-0.11	0.08	-0.17	0.07	1	0.19	-0.06	-0.04	0.02	0.22	0.05	0.05	-0.03	0.12	-0.11	0.13	0.10	0.20
Refugees Origin	-0.03	0.00	-0.03	-0.05	-0.04	0.09	0.16	-0.04	0.19	0.05	0.21	0.19	1	-0.14	0.21	-0.21	0.08	-0.16	-0.07	-0.04	0.22	-0.13	-0.07	-0.05	0.21
GDP per Capita	-0.05	-0.01	-0.02	-0.03	0.16	0.00	-0.59	0.07	-0.53	-0.18	-0.46	-0.06	-0.14	1	-0.52	0.48	-0.18	0.58	0.28	-0.26	-0.43	0.35	0.14	0.02	-0.37
Infant Mortality	0.02	0.04	0.08	0.12	-0.13	0.39	0.59	-0.03	0.87	0.53	0.85	-0.04	0.21	-0.52	1	-0.83	-0.01	-0.93	-0.22	0.20	0.47	-0.39	-0.36	-0.15	0.24
Improved Water	-0.05	-0.07	-0.15	-0.25	0.13	-0.37	-0.60	0.02	-0.81	-0.34	-0.81	0.02	-0.21	0.48	-0.83	1	0.05	0.75	0.22	-0.19	-0.47	0.43	0.27	0.12	-0.23
Unemployment	-0.02	0.01	0.05	0.11	-0.09	-0.20	-0.01	0.02	-0.05	0.16	-0.06	0.22	0.08	-0.18	-0.01	0.05	1	-0.09	0.06	-0.29	-0.04	0.04	0.11	0.08	-0.07
Life Expectancy	-0.01	-0.04	-0.08	-0.13	0.16	-0.35	-0.62	-0.01	-0.62	-0.62	-0.82	0.05	-0.16	0.58	-0.93	0.75	-0.09	1	0.19	-0.13	-0.47	0.40	0.32	0.21	-0.19
Trade	0.02	-0.03	-0.03	-0.04	0.52	-0.02	-0.11	-0.16	-0.24	-0.09	-0.25	0.03	-0.07	0.28	-0.22	0.22	0.06	0.19	1	-0.08	-0.07	0.02	0.03	-0.07	-0.17
Caloric intake	0.05	-0.01	-0.04	-0.07	0.20	0.18	0.28	-0.23	0.16	-0.23	0.12	-0.03	-0.04	-0.26	0.20	-0.19	-0.29	-0.13	-0.08	1	0.26	-0.21	-0.13	0.03	0.28
Freedom	0.12	0.09	0.13	0.15	-0.01	0.42	0.33	-0.07	0.48	0.00	0.43	0.12	0.22	-0.43	0.47	-0.47	-0.04	-0.47	-0.07	0.26	1	-0.89	-0.11	-0.02	0.50
Polity IV	-0.13	-0.11	-0.12	-0.13	-0.06	-0.47	-0.30	0.08	-0.43	0.09	-0.39	-0.11	-0.13	0.35	-0.39	0.43	0.04	0.40	0.02	-0.21	-0.89	1	0.11	0.06	-0.49
Ethnic Diversity	0	-0.03	-0.05	-0.06	0.01	-0.36	-0.15	0.04	-0.36	-0.09	-0.36	0.13	-0.07	0.14	-0.36	0.27	0.11	0.32	0.03	-0.13	-0.11	0.11	1	0.10	-0.13
Religious Diversity	0.00	0	-0.01	0.02	-0.08	0.00	-0.19	-0.08	-0.11	-0.27	-0.14	0.10	-0.05	0.02	-0.15	0.12	0.08	0.21	-0.07	0.03	-0.02	0.06	0.10	1	0.13
Border Conflict	0.12	0.03	0	0.02	0.05	0.30	0.24	-0.10	0.30	-0.26	0.25	0.20	0.21	-0.37	0.24	-0.23	-0.07	-0.19	-0.17	0.28	0.50	-0.49	-0.13	0.13	1

Table 11: Correlation Heat Map after Removing Variables

	HIIK Trend	2 Yr Freedom Trend	3 Yr Freedom Trend	5 yr Freedom Trend	Pop density	Pop growth	Rural Pop	Arable land	Death Rate	Refugees Asylum	Refugees Origin	GDP per Capita	Infant Mortality	Improved Water	Unemployment	Trade	Caloric intake	Freedom	Polity IV	Ethnic Diversity	Religious Diversity	Border Conflict
HIIK Trend	1	-0.04	0.00	0.00	-0.01	0.07	0.00	-0.04	-0.08	0.05	-0.03	-0.05	0.02	-0.05	-0.02	0.02	0.05	0.12	-0.13	0.02	0.00	0.12
2 Yr Freedom Trend	-0.04	1	0.71	0.55	-0.05	0.07	-0.03	-0.02	-0.01	0.05	0.00	-0.01	0.04	-0.07	0.01	-0.03	-0.01	0.09	-0.11	-0.03	-0.02	0.03
3 Yr Freedom Trend	0.00	0.71	1	0.78	-0.07	0.10	-0.03	-0.01	0.02	0.09	-0.03	-0.02	0.08	-0.15	0.05	-0.03	-0.04	0.13	-0.12	-0.05	-0.01	0.04
5 yr Freedom Trend	0.00	0.55	0.78	1	-0.11	0.13	-0.03	0.01	0.06	0.16	-0.05	-0.03	0.12	-0.25	0.11	-0.04	-0.07	0.15	-0.13	-0.06	0.02	0.02
Pop density	-0.01	-0.05	-0.07	-0.11	1	0.04	-0.05	-0.17	-0.16	0.04	-0.04	0.16	-0.13	0.13	-0.09	0.52	0.20	-0.01	-0.06	0.01	-0.08	0.05
Pop growth	0.07	0.07	0.10	0.13	0.04	1	0.13	-0.15	-0.18	0.08	0.09	0.00	0.39	-0.37	-0.20	-0.02	0.18	0.42	-0.47	-0.36	0.00	0.30
Rural Pop	0.00	-0.03	-0.03	-0.03	-0.05	0.13	1	-0.11	0.27	-0.12	0.16	-0.59	0.59	-0.60	-0.01	-0.11	0.28	0.33	-0.30	-0.15	-0.19	0.24
Arable land	-0.04	-0.02	-0.01	0.01	-0.17	-0.15	-0.11	1	0.27	-0.11	-0.04	0.07	-0.03	0.02	0.02	-0.16	-0.23	-0.07	0.08	0.04	-0.08	-0.10
Death Rate	-0.08	-0.01	0.02	0.06	-0.16	-0.18	0.27	0.27	1	-0.17	0.05	-0.18	0.53	-0.34	0.16	-0.09	-0.23	0.00	0.09	-0.09	-0.27	-0.26
Refugees Asylum	0.05	0.05	0.09	0.16	0.04	0.08	-0.12	-0.11	-0.17	1	0.19	-0.06	-0.04	0.02	0.22	0.05	-0.03	0.12	-0.11	0.13	0.10	0.20
Refugees Origin	-0.03	0.00	-0.03	-0.05	-0.04	0.09	0.16	-0.04	0.05	0.19	1	-0.14	0.21	-0.21	0.08	-0.07	-0.04	0.22	-0.13	-0.07	-0.05	0.21
GDP per Capita	-0.05	-0.01	-0.02	-0.03	0.16	0.00	-0.59	0.07	-0.18	-0.06	-0.14	1	-0.52	0.48	-0.18	0.28	-0.26	-0.43	0.35	0.14	0.02	-0.37
Infant Mortality	0.02	0.04	0.08	0.12	-0.13	0.39	0.59	-0.03	0.53	-0.04	0.21	-0.52	1	-0.83	-0.01	-0.22	0.20	0.47	-0.39	-0.36	-0.15	0.24
Improved Water	-0.05	-0.07	-0.15	-0.25	0.13	-0.37	-0.60	0.02	-0.34	0.02	-0.21	0.48	-0.83	1	0.05	0.22	-0.19	-0.47	0.43	0.27	0.12	-0.23
Unemployment	-0.02	0.01	0.05	0.11	-0.09	-0.20	-0.01	0.02	0.16	0.22	0.08	-0.18	-0.01	0.05	1	0.06	-0.29	-0.04	0.04	0.11	0.08	-0.07
Trade	0.02	-0.03	-0.03	-0.04	0.52	-0.02	-0.11	-0.16	-0.09	0.03	-0.07	0.28	-0.22	0.22	0.06	1	-0.08	-0.07	0.02	0.03	-0.07	-0.17
Caloric intake	0.05	-0.01	-0.04	-0.07	0.20	0.18	0.28	-0.23	-0.23	-0.03	-0.04	-0.26	0.20	-0.19	-0.29	-0.08	1	0.26	-0.21	-0.13	0.03	0.28
Freedom	0.12	0.09	0.13	0.15	-0.01	0.42	0.33	-0.07	0.00	0.12	0.22	-0.43	0.47	-0.47	-0.04	-0.07	0.26	1	-0.89	-0.11	-0.02	0.50
Polity IV	-0.13	-0.11	-0.12	-0.13	-0.06	-0.47	-0.30	0.08	0.09	-0.11	-0.13	0.35	-0.39	0.43	0.04	0.02	-0.21	-0.89	1	0.11	0.06	-0.49
Ethnic Diversity	0.02	-0.03	-0.05	-0.06	0.01	-0.36	-0.15	0.04	-0.09	0.13	-0.07	0.14	-0.36	0.27	0.11	0.03	-0.13	-0.11	0.11	1	0.10	-0.13
Religious Diversity	0.00	-0.02	-0.01	0.02	-0.08	0.00	-0.19	-0.08	-0.27	0.10	-0.05	0.02	-0.15	0.12	0.08	-0.07	0.03	-0.02	0.06	0.10	1	0.13
Border Conflict	0.12	0.03	0.04	0.02	0.05	0.30	0.24	-0.10	-0.26	0.20	0.21	-0.37	0.24	-0.23	-0.07	-0.17	0.28	0.50	-0.49	-0.13	0.13	1

Model building set and Validation Set

For the initial analysis, a model for 2011 and 2012 is developed and 2013 data is used to validate. Before the model can be built, the missing data needs to be imputed (filled in). For the 2011-2013 model and validation database only 345 out of 546 nations have data for all 23 variables. Unfortunately, often the nations with the worst data are the ones in the most danger of being in conflict. On average, a nation has 22.1 variables out of 23. The nation with the worst data is understandably South Sudan which is the world's newest nation, gaining independence in 2006. This fledgling and tumultuous nation does not yet have the data infrastructure necessary for good data collection. Table 12 shows the nations with the worst data, ones that have complete data for 20 or fewer variables.

Table 12: Number of Variables per Nation; Nations with Worst Data

Country	Number of Variables		
	2011	2012	2013
South Sudan	12	12	13
Micronesia (Federated States of)	17	17	16
Tonga	17	17	17
West Bank and Gaza	17	17	17
Kiribati	18	18	18
Seychelles	18	18	18
Vanuatu	18	18	19
Antigua and Barbuda	19	19	19
Comoros	19	19	19
Grenada	19	19	19
Samoa	19	18	19
Sao Tome and Principe	19	19	19
Timor-Leste	19	19	19
Bahamas	20	20	21
Barbados	20	20	20
Brunei Darussalam	20	20	20
Democratic People's Republic of Korea	20	20	20
Equatorial Guinea	20	20	20
Maldives	20	20	20
Myanmar	20	20	20
Singapore	20	20	20
Solomon Islands	20	20	20
Somalia	20	20	20

Data Imputation

The JMP software offers a method to impute data. Imputing analyzes similar values in other columns and rows to estimate the missing value (Hinrichs, 2010). JMP produces a new data table that duplicates the data table and replaces all missing values with estimated values (SAS Institute, 2015). Imputed values are expectations conditional on the non-missing values for each row. The mean and covariance matrix is used for the imputation calculation.

Methods to develop the Model

A method is needed to construct models now that the dependent and independent variables have been identified, screened and compiled into a model and validation dataset. Three method are introduced; two correlation methods and a least significant method. Models will be constructed using all methods and tested against each other using the Validation set prediction accuracy as the grading requirement.

Method 1: Correlation method

The correlation method will start with zero variables and add variables based upon significance. The variables with the highest correlation with the HIIK intensity levels will be tested first for inclusion in the model and no variables will be removed once they have been included. Table 13shows the variable correlations with the HIIK intensity level used for the testing order with this method. The correlation for regime type, which is nominal, is acquired by assigning values to the regime types (Democratic =1, Central ruler/ruling party = 2, Emerging, transitional, recent change, Disputed = 3).

42

Table 13: Correlation with HIIK Intensity Level

Order for Testing	Variable	HIIK Intensity Level Correlation
1	Freedom	0.49
2	Polity IV	-0.37
3	Border Conflict	0.33
4	Improved Water	-0.32
5	GDP per Capita	-0.32
6	Trade	-0.29
7	Infant Mortality	0.27
8	Regime Type	0.23
9	Refugees Origin	0.17
10	Rural Pop	0.16
11	Caloric intake	0.15
12	Pop growth	0.14
13	Religious Diversity	0.13
14	HIIK Trend	0.09
15	Ethnic Diversity	-0.07
16	Pop density	-0.06
17	Unemployment	-0.03
18	Refugees Asylum	-0.03
19	5 yr Freedom Trend	0.03
20	Death Rate	-0.02
21	2 Yr Freedom Trend	-0.02
22	Arable land	0.01
23	3 Yr Freedom Trend	0.00

Method 2: Alternate correlation method

An alternate version of the correlation method is to remove variables if they reach an alpha greater than .10, using a hypothesis test. The 2nd order polynomials for the three main effects with the greatest significance are also tested for inclusion.

Method 3: Remove the least significant variable

This method will begin with all 23 variables and remove the least significant variable. The Effect Likelihood Ratio Test will be used to determine the least significant variable. One insignificant variable will be removed at a time and the model will be tested again to determine the next insignificant variable to remove. The prediction accuracy will be saved for each iteration in order to build the Signal to Noise Ratio chart described in chapter 4. The prediction accuracy is calculated using the formula in Figure 6.

Alternate Model: Only nations that enter into a violent conflict

Three methods were investigated to analyze only nations that are new to violent conflict. The first method uses a new database from 2009-2013, one that only includes nations that entered into violent conflict and their corresponding row of data from the previous year. The goal for this method is to build a model that predicts the year the nation transitions into violent conflict. The dependent variable remained the same as before except now the database was substantially smaller, only using nations new to conflict and their previous year. Twenty independent variables were considered. The three locked variables were omitted because they did not change between the years.

For the 2nd method a database was compiled of new nations to violent conflict in addition to previous years when the nation was in a state of "Not violent conflict". Similar to method 1, this method differs in that only nations with a period of "not in violent conflict" for at least 2 consecutive years before the transition to violence were included. The goal was to have a distinct period of "not violent conflict" years and then the "violent conflict" year. The alternate correlation method was used to construct a model and test for variable significance.

The 3rd method involved analyzing the behavior of false positives and false negatives in the four years following their false prediction. The premise is that the model believes they should be in conflict so they are likely candidates for conflict the next year or soon after. Nations falsely predicted will be analyzed the following years to determine the likelihood they will eventually transition to a violent conflict. This method will also look at different logistic probabilities. Recall the output of logistic regression is a probability that is rounded to either 0 or 1 using a threshold value with a default of .5. The higher the probability is, the more certain the model is that the nation will be in a violent conflict. A nation with a probability of .8 can be translated as the model is 80% certain the nation will be in a state of violent conflict for its predicted year. The study further analyzes nations at different probability levels. This method assumes the state of the nation remains constant over the future analyzed years.

Summary

Methodologies have been described for logistic regression, model building, sensitivity analysis and methods to predict nations new to violent conflict. The dependent variable has been defined. The independent variables have been defined and screened. Two separate databases (2011-2013 & 2009-2013) have been constructed and missing data imputed. The next step uses these methods and data to construct models and conduct analysis.

IV. Analysis and Results

Chapter Overview

This chapter will use the methods described previously to construct trial models. These trial models will be assigned a name, such as Trial Model 1, and be compared to each other using the validation set prediction accuracy as the test for model goodness. The initial analysis is conducted using a database from 2011-2013. Two years are set aside to build the model (2011-2012) and one year is used to validate the model (2013). A few of the independent variables restrict the size of the database. After initial analysis these variables are removed from consideration and the database is allowed to expand. The second set of analysis uses a database from 2009-2013. Three years are set aside to build the model (2009-2011) and two years are used to validate the model (2012-2013). Factor Analysis and robustness of the confusion matrix cut off value are explored to gain insight on the problem.

Results of Constructing Logistic Regression Trial Models
Method 1 - Correlation Method

The process described in chapter 3 is used for all the variables in the order listed in

Table 13. Using this method, seven variables are accepted into the model at an alpha = .1 and six variables are accepted at an alpha = .05. The variable accepted at alpha = .1 and not at alpha = .05 is "2 yr Freedom trend". A model of all the variables significant at alpha = .1 is shown below in Figure 9. This model will be called Trial

Model 1. Also included in Figure 10 is a graph showing the contribution of each significant variable at an alpha = .1, a confusion matrix for the training set and the JMP output for the whole model. Figure 10 shows the same information for the variables significant at an alpha = .05. This model will be called Trial Model 2. These models are set aside for later validation.

Trial Model 1

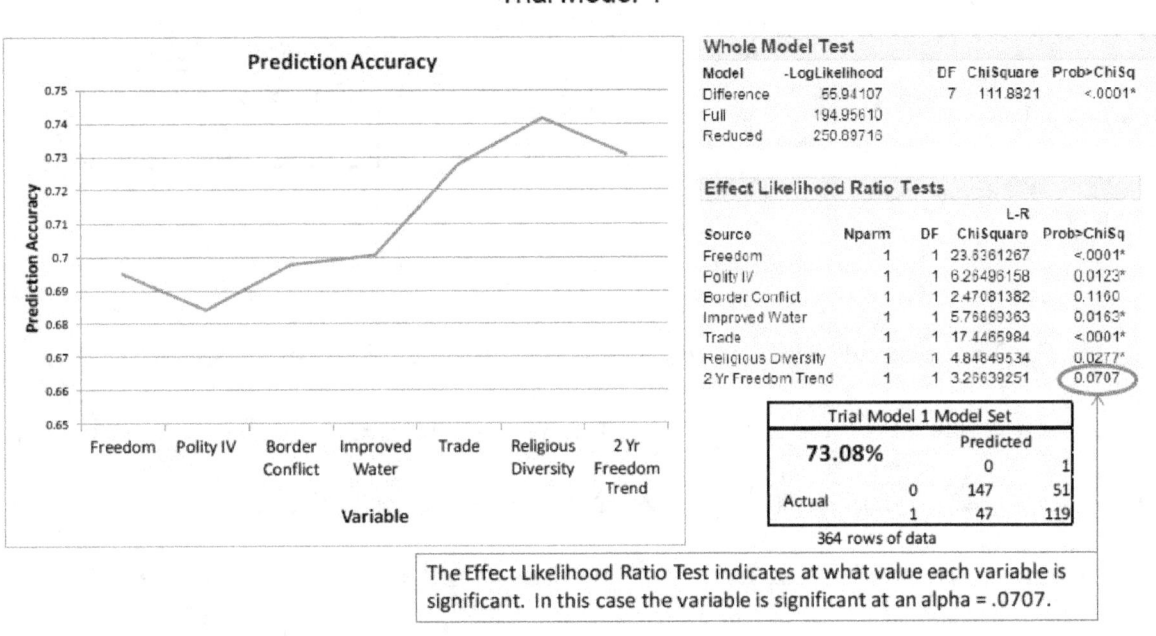

Figure 9: Trial Model 1 Output

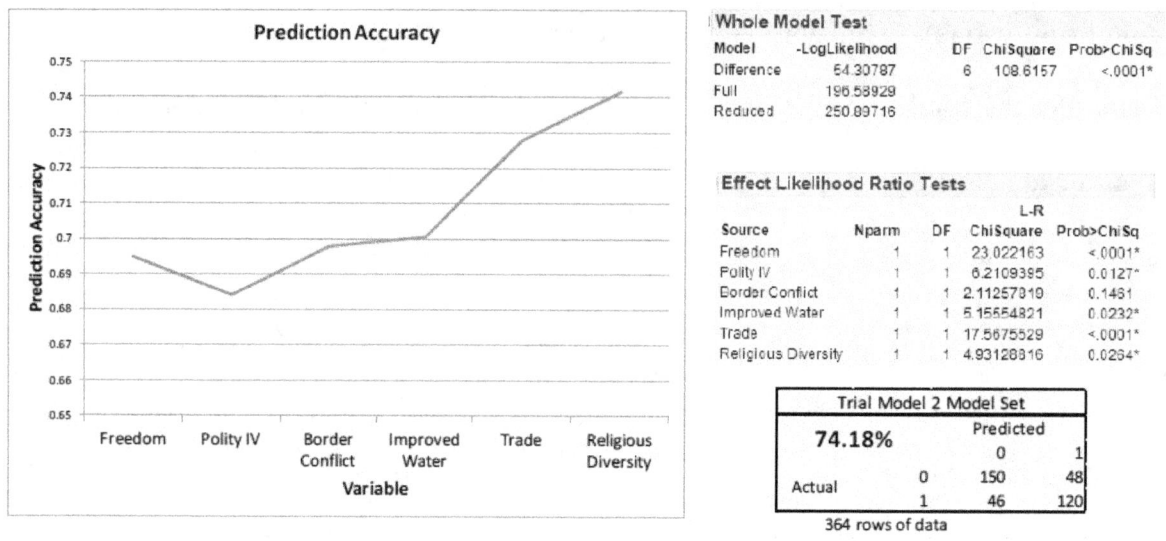

Figure 10: Trial Model 2 Output

For Figure 9 and Figure 10 the Effect Likelihood Ratio Tests indicates at what value each variable is significant for this sample. As variables are added, the significance of the previously added variables change. Note, the Border Conflict variable was added because it was originally significant at an alpha = .05 but as additional variables are added the Border Conflict significance decreases below the alpha = .1 threshold. This method does not remove variables once they have been included so Border Conflict remains in the model. Method two will remove these variables. Trial Model 1 and 2 only include main effect variables. 2nd order polynomials are next tested for significance. 2nd order polynomials can help explain some non-linear effects. Trial Model 3 includes main effects at alpha = .1 and their 2nd order polynomials. A model using an alpha = .05 threshold shows negligible difference to Trial Model 3 so it is not included in the analysis.

Polynomials are tested in the same order as main effects; see Table 13, using the same hypothesis tests. Polynomials can model a non-linear relationship between the dependent and independent variables. The results of this process are shown in Figure 11. Only Freedom*Freedom was added to the model. Water*Water was near the threshold, having a value of .1005 for Trial Model 3. A detailed description of one of the trial models is provided in a later section.

Trial Model 3

Whole Model Test

Model	-LogLikelihood	DF	ChiSquare	Prob>ChiSq
Difference	60.75900	8	121.518	<.0001*
Full	190.13817			
Reduced	250.89716			

Effect Likelihood Ratio Tests

Source	Nparm	DF	L-R ChiSquare	Prob>ChiSq
Freedom	1	1	27.7790716	<.0001*
Polity IV	1	1	4.76398229	0.0291*
Border Conflict	1	1	1.20790963	0.2717
Improved Water	1	1	2.77698683	0.0956
Trade	1	1	18.0281343	<.0001*
Religious Diversity	1	1	2.5419449	0.1109
2 Yr Freedom Trend	1	1	2.97938677	0.0843
Freedom*Freedom	1	1	9.6358629	0.0019*

Trial Model 3 Model Set			
74.18%		Predicted	
		0	1
Actual	0	143	55
	1	39	127

364 rows of data

Figure 11: Trial Model 3

49

Method 2 – Alternate Correlation Method

Variables were tested in the same order as method 1 but variables were removed when their alpha value was greater than 0.1. 2nd order polynomials were also tested in the same order. Trial Model 4 was constructed using this method and is shown in Figure 12.

Trial Model 4

Whole Model Test

Model	-LogLikelihood	DF	ChiSquare	Prob>ChiSq
Difference	56.70358	4	113.4072	<.0001*
Full	194.19358			
Reduced	250.89716			

Effect Likelihood Ratio Tests

Source	Nparm	DF	L-R ChiSquare	Prob>ChiSq
Freedom	1	1	35.2927739	<.0001*
Polity IV	1	1	4.12362338	0.0423*
Trade	1	1	24.4648079	<.0001*
Freedom*Freedom	1	1	16.265552	<.0001*

Trial Model 4 Model Set			
73.63%		Predicted	
		0	1
Actual	0	139	59
	1	37	129

364 rows of data

Figure 12: Trial Model 4

Method 3 - Least Significant Variable Method

Method 3, starting with all of the variables and removing the least significant one until they are all significant at a certain threshold, is used to construct the next 5 models. The Signal to Noise Ratio Chart, shown in Figure 13, is calculated using the prediction accuracy for each iteration of removing a variable. These charts show the impact each variable has on the model set prediction accuracy. For example, the variables from Trial

Model 5 have a prediction accuracy of .747. Removing the variable "2 yr Freedom

Trend" variable has no effect on the prediction accuracy but additionally removing the

variable "Rural population" decreases the prediction accuracy to 0.73. Two Models are

used from this process; Trial Model 5 includes all main effects significant at an alpha = .1

and Trial Model 6 includes all main effects significant at an alpha = .05. The results from

Trial Model 5 and 6 are shown in Figure 14 and a signal to noise ratio chart from this

process is shown in Figure 13.

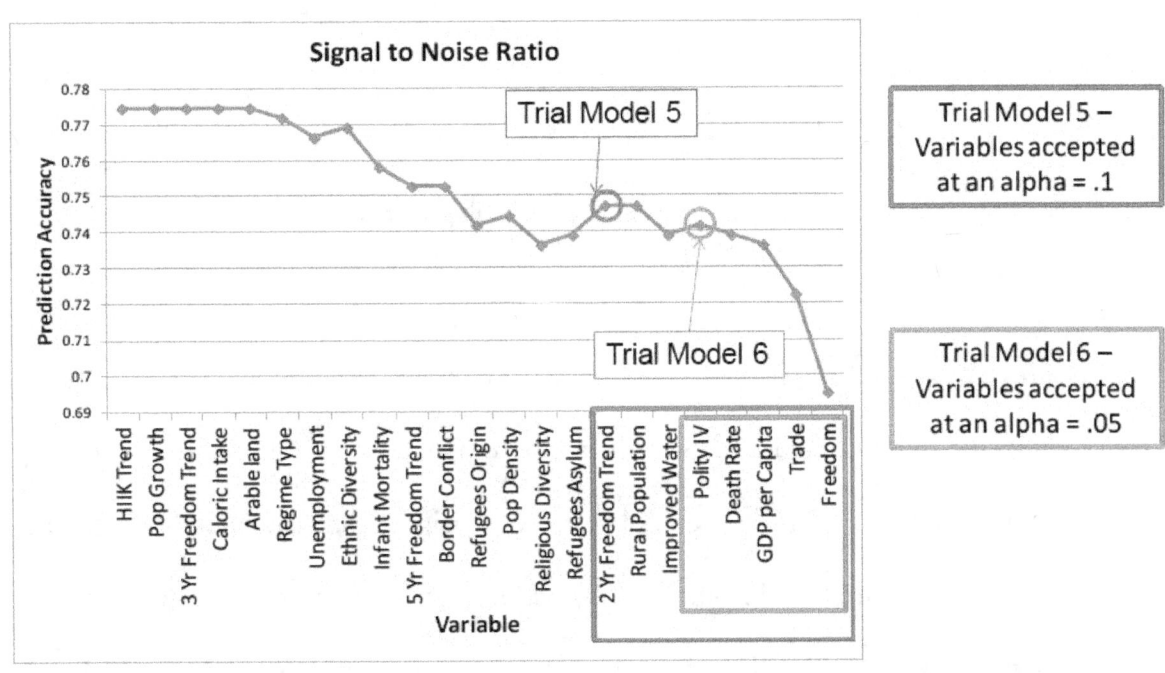

Figure 13: Signal to Noise Ratio, Trial Model 5 & 6

Trial Model 5

Whole Model Test

Model	-LogLikelihood	DF	ChiSquare	Prob>ChiSq
Difference	59.02382	8	118.0476	<.0001*
Full	191.87334			
Reduced	250.89716			

Effect Likelihood Ratio Tests

Source	Nparm	DF	L-R ChiSquare	Prob>ChiSq
2 Yr Freedom Trend	1	1	3.70553302	0.0542
Rural Pop	1	1	3.74814145	0.0529
Death Rate	1	1	6.77658746	0.0092*
GDP per Capita	1	1	6.9761947	0.0083*
Improved Water	1	1	6.83746402	0.0089*
Trade	1	1	18.4000739	<.0001*
Freedom	1	1	22.403715	<.0001*
Polity IV	1	1	6.68427701	0.0097*

Trial Model 5 Model Set			
74.73%		Predicted	
		0	1
Actual	0	148	50
	1	42	124

364 rows of data

Trial Model 6

Whole Model Test

Model	-LogLikelihood	DF	ChiSquare	Prob>ChiSq
Difference	53.98055	5	107.9611	<.0001*
Full	196.91661			
Reduced	250.89716			

Effect Likelihood Ratio Tests

Source	Nparm	DF	L-R ChiSquare	Prob>ChiSq
Death Rate	1	1	4.46802559	0.0345*
GDP per Capita	1	1	8.61984227	0.0033*
Trade	1	1	23.022032	<.0001*
Freedom	1	1	21.0752319	<.0001*
Polity IV	1	1	4.39645499	0.0360*

Trial Model 6 Model Set			
74.18%		Predicted	
		0	1
Actual	0	147	51
	1	43	123

364 rows of data

Figure 14: Trial Models 5 & 6

All variables in Trial Model 5 and Trial Model 6 are raised to a 2nd order Polynomial and tested in the same "least significant" method. Hierarchy is enforced, a main effect will not be removed if its 2nd order polynomial is insignificant and included in the model. Three models are saved from this process, the results are shown in Figure 15 and the Signal to Noise Ratio Charts are shown in Figure 16 and Figure 17. Trial Model 7 includes all main effects and 2nd order polynomials from Trial Model 5 that are significant at an alpha = .05, with the exception of one of the main effects. In this case GDP per capita has an Effects Likelihood Ratio Test value of .32 but its 2nd order polynomial has a value of .018. Trial Model 8 includes all main effects and 2nd order polynomials from Trial Model 5 that are significant at an alpha = .05, without exception.

Trial Model 9 includes all main effects and 2nd order polynomials from Trial Model 6 that are significant at an alpha = .05.

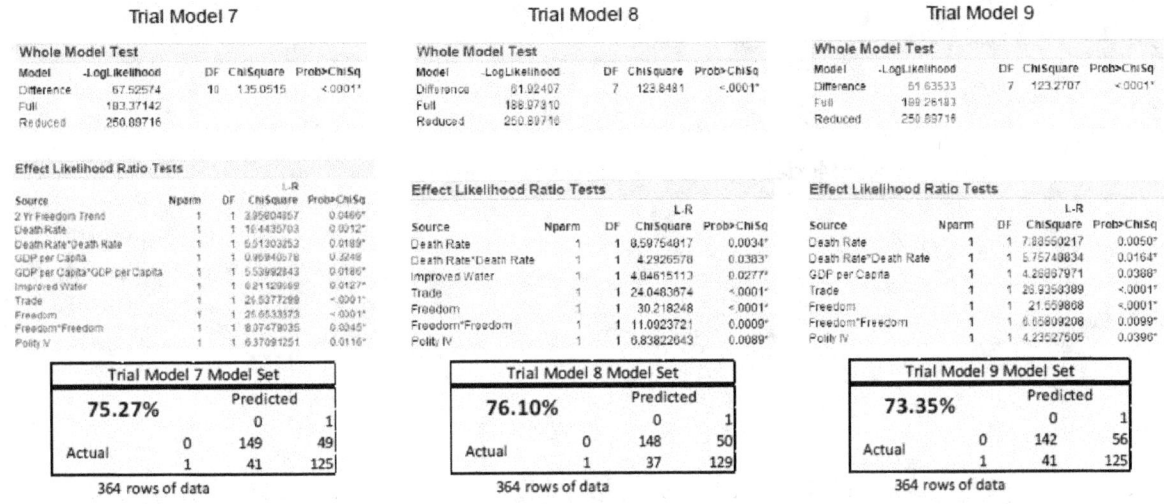

Figure 15: Trial Models 7, 8 & 9

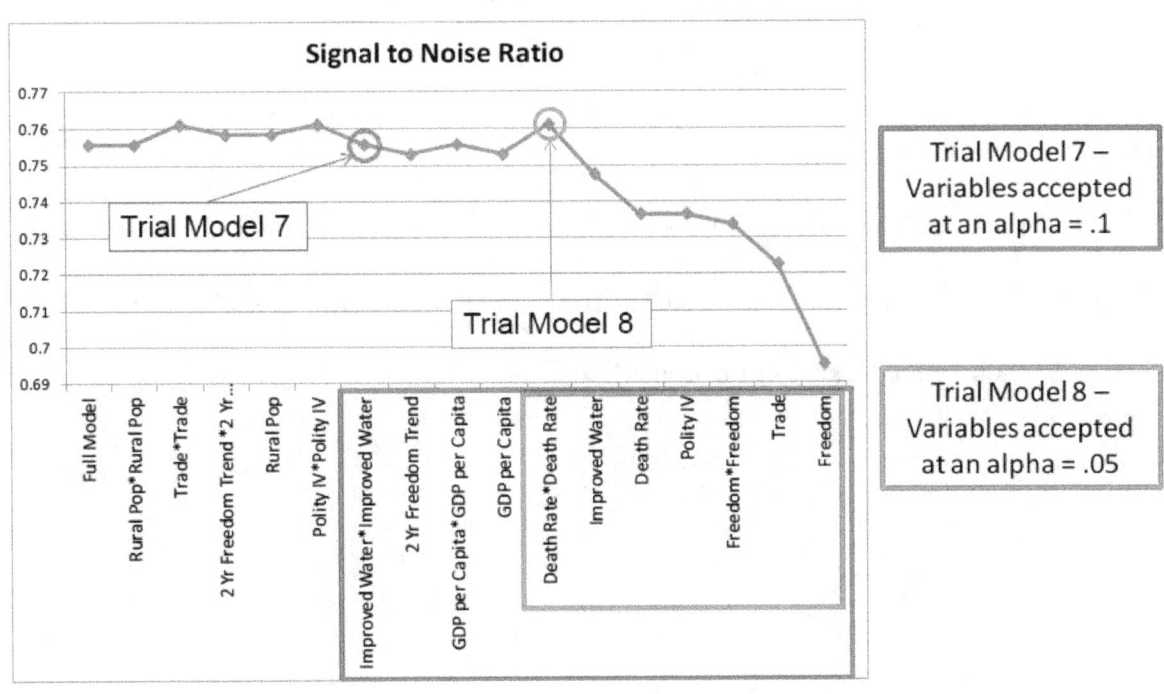

Figure 16: Signal to Noise Ratio, Trial Model 7 & 8

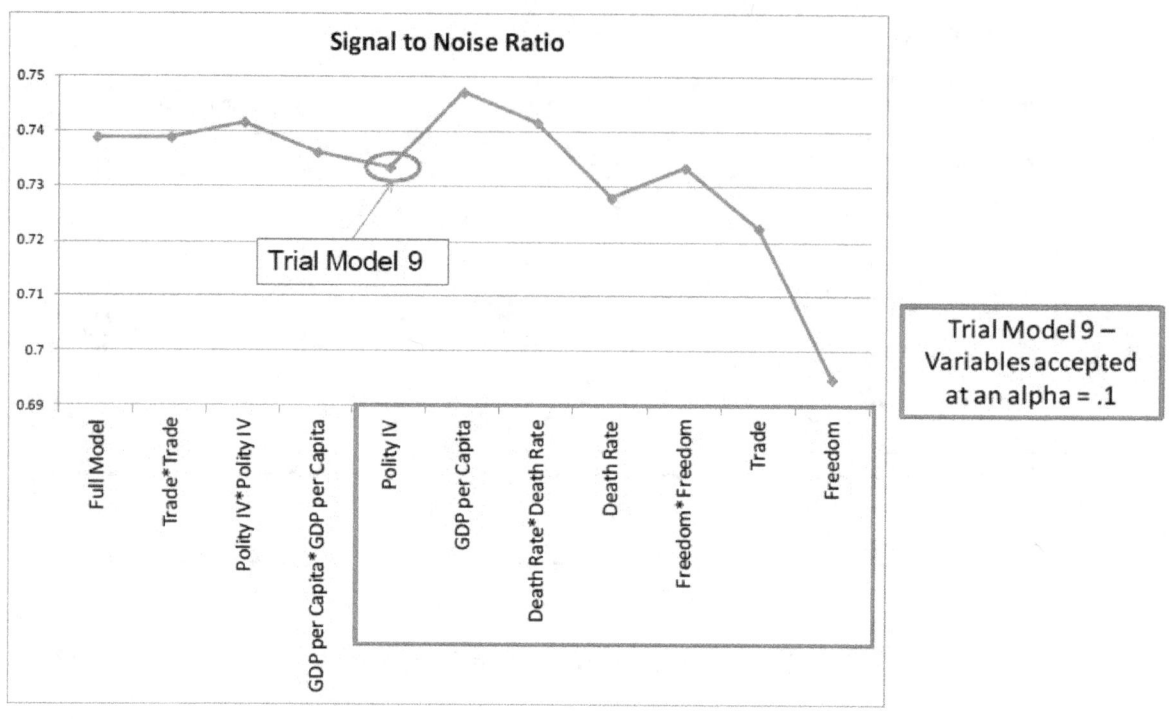

Figure 17: Signal to Noise Ratio, Trial Model 9

Results of the Trial Models

All nine trial models were tested with the 2013 validation data and the results are shown in Table 14. The two best models (Trial Model 5 and Trial Model 7) were constructed using the least significant method.

Table 14: Trial Model Prediction Accuracy

			Prediction Accuracy		
Construction Method	Trial Model #	Num of Variables	Model Set	Validation Set	Model and Validation Set
Method 1 - Correlation Method	1	7	73.1%	72.0%	72.7%
	2	6	74.2%	71.4%	73.3%
	3	8	74.2%	74.2%	74.2%
Method 2 - Alternate	4	4	73.6%	73.1%	73.4%
Method 3 - Least Significant Method	5	8	74.7%	74.7%	74.7%
	6	5	74.2%	72.0%	73.4%
	7	10	75.3%	76.4%	75.6%
	8	7	76.1%	72.5%	74.9%
	9	7	73.4%	73.1%	74.9%

Trial Model 7 has the best validation set prediction accuracy. This is also the only model whose prediction accuracy is greater in the validation set than in the model set, indicating a good fit. Trial Model 7 has 10 variables, including six main effects, one trend variable and three 2nd order polynomials. Statistical results for Trial Model 7 were previously shown in Figure 15.

The coefficients for Trial Model 7 are shown in Table 15. The main effects are listed in order of significance, as determined by their effect likelihood ratio test statistic. It is important to note that the variable data was not normalized, which explains the large variety in the values of the coefficients.

Table 15: Coefficients for Trial Model 7

β_0 Intercept	β_1 Trade	β_2 Freedom	β_3 Death Rate	β_4 Polity IV	β_5 Improved Water	β_6 2 yr Freedom trend	β_7 GDP per Capita	β_8 Freedom^2	β_9 GDP per Capita^2	β_{10} Death Rate^2
-1.337	0.020	-0 817	0.150	-0.190	0.027	7.033	-2.23E-05	0.133	1.52E-09	-0.023

Recall the logit transformation function in Equation 3. The coefficients in Table 15 are multiplied by the nations' applicable data to attain the logit. The probability of a nation entering into a violent conflict is attained from the logit function. The values of the coefficients explain the effect the variable has on the probability of violent conflict. A positive coefficient for a main effect means that as the variable increases, the probability of a violent conflict decreases. A negative coefficient for a main effect means that as a variable increases, the probability of a violent conflict increases. Table 15 can be interpreted as reading; as a nation's Trade, Death Rate, percent living near improved water and 2 year freedom trend decrease, its probability of violent conflict increase. Likewise, as a nations Freedom score (less is better), Polity IV score (less is better) and GDP per Capita increase, so does its probability of violent conflict. This is intuitive for all variables except for Death Rate and GDP per Capita. For these variables their 2nd order polynomials provide the explanation. The polynomial variables can be interpreted as reading; as nation's Death Rate increase, so does its probability of violent conflict and as a nation's GDP per capita decrease, its probability of violent conflict increases. All of the variables contribute to the model in an expected manner.

The validation set prediction accuracy for Trial Model 7 is shown in Figure 18. This model will serve as the baseline for further analysis. Note the balanced number of false predictions, 22 false negatives and 21 false positives. The sensitivity of the false predictions is examined in a following section.

Trial Model 7 Validation Set			
76.37%		Predicted	
		0	1
Actual	0	70	21
	1	22	69

182 rows of data

Figure 18: Trial Model 7 Test Set Prediction Accuracy

Factor Analysis and Noise Reduction Techniques

Factor Analysis is a method to replace the observable variables with fewer unobservable factors. Factor Analysis can reduce the 23 variables that pass initial screening to a few factors. Variables with high correlation with each other can be represented as a single factor. This is useful because it can help identify outliers and lend insight to the data set. Data from 2011-2013 database with182 nations per year is used to conduct the factor analysis. First it is necessary to determine the number of factors to analyze. A Scree plot, shown in Figure 19, of Principal Component Eigenvalues is used to determine the appropriate number of factors that should be considered. The number of factors to analyze is equal to the number of Principal Components that have eigenvalues greater than the corresponding Horn's Curve value (Horn, 1965). The Horn's curve values are estimated using 100 Monte Carlo iterations (Bigley, 2013).

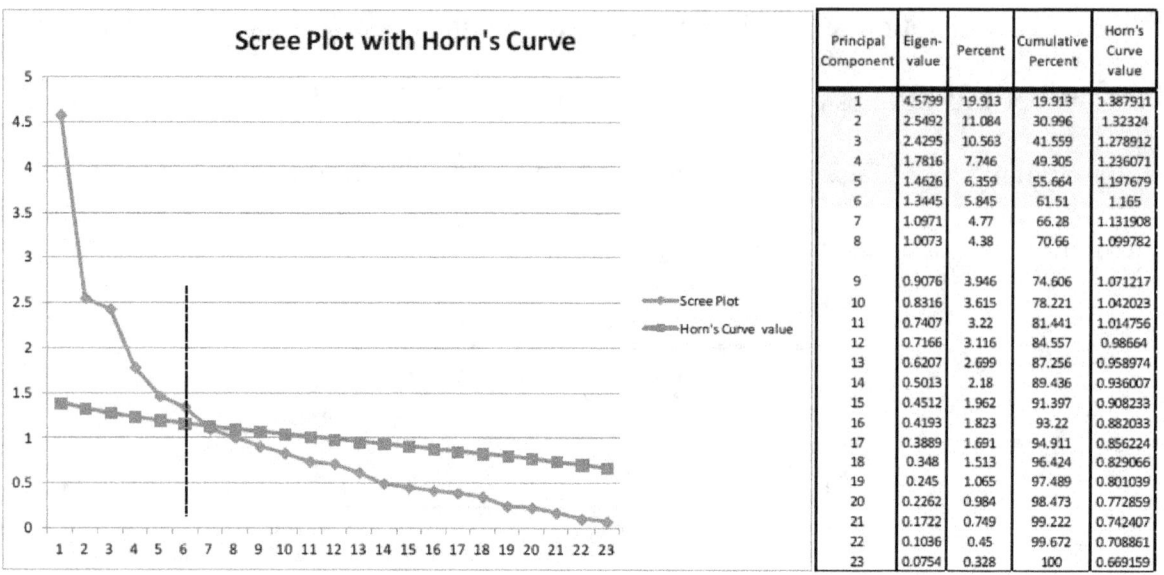

Principal Component	Eigen-value	Percent	Cumulative Percent	Horn's Curve value
1	4.5799	19.913	19.913	1.387911
2	2.5492	11.084	30.996	1.32324
3	2.4295	10.563	41.559	1.278912
4	1.7816	7.746	49.305	1.236071
5	1.4626	6.359	55.664	1.197679
6	1.3445	5.845	61.51	1.165
7	1.0971	4.77	66.28	1.131908
8	1.0073	4.38	70.66	1.099782
9	0.9076	3.946	74.606	1.071217
10	0.8316	3.615	78.221	1.042023
11	0.7407	3.22	81.441	1.014756
12	0.7166	3.116	84.557	0.98664
13	0.6207	2.699	87.256	0.958974
14	0.5013	2.18	89.436	0.936007
15	0.4512	1.962	91.397	0.908233
16	0.4193	1.823	93.22	0.882033
17	0.3889	1.691	94.911	0.856224
18	0.348	1.513	96.424	0.829066
19	0.245	1.065	97.489	0.801039
20	0.2262	0.984	98.473	0.772859
21	0.1722	0.749	99.222	0.742407
22	0.1036	0.45	99.672	0.708861
23	0.0754	0.328	100	0.669159

Figure 19: Scree Plot and Horn's Curve

In this case six factors are relevant for analysis. JMP software is used to compute the Factor Analysis using a Varimax rotation. Table 16 shows the loadings score for each variable and each factor. Higher loading scores indicate a variable is highly correlated to a factor.

Table 16: Factor Loadings and Variance Explained

Variable	Factor 1	Factor 2	Factor 3	Factor 4	Factor 5	Factor 6
HIIK Trend	0	0.20	-0.03	0.15	-0.04	-0.03
2 Yr Freedom Trend	-0.01	0	0.82	0.02	-0.02	0.00
3 Yr Freedom Trend	0.02	0.02	1	0.00	0.01	-0.02
5 yr Freedom Trend	0.06	0.06	0.88	0	0.06	-0.05
Pop density	-0.06	0.00	-0.07	0.12	0	0.82
Pop growth	0.11	0.52	0.16	0.09	-0.55	0
Rural Pop	0.82	0.04	-0.08	0.05	-0.04	0.05
Arable land	-0.13	0.00	-0.05	-0.50	-0.04	-0.38
Death Rate	0.50	-0.20	0.01	-0.67	0.09	-0.09
Refugees Asylum	-0.08	0.37	0.18	0.17	0.48	0.06
Refugees Origin	0.19	0.44	-0.08	-0.13	0.22	-0.04
GDP per Capita	-0.79	-0.09	0.02	-0.27	-0.19	0.18
Infant Mortality	0.83	0.22	0.08	-0.18	-0.23	-0.10
Improved Water	-0.76	-0.29	-0.17	0.15	0.23	0.09
Unemployment	0.13	0.01	0.10	-0.12	0.74	0.00
Trade	-0.19	0.00	0.00	-0.09	0.08	0.81
Caloric intake	0.30	0.05	-0.07	0.54	-0.34	0.25
Freedom	0.40	0.77	0.11	0.12	-0.09	0.00
Polity IV	-0.30	-0.80	-0.09	-0.10	0.14	-0.05
Regime Type	-0.21	0.75	-0.02	-0.06	0.17	0.05
Ethnic Diversity	-0.28	-0.02	-0.08	0.05	0.53	-0.01
Religious Diversity	-0.19	-0.04	0.02	0.54	0.18	-0.28
Border Conflict	0	0.47	0.01	0.51	-0.07	-0.08

Variance Explained			
Factor	Variance	Percent	Cumulative Percent
Factor 1	3.5091	15.257	15.257
Factor 2	2.8494	12.389	27.646
Factor 3	2.4802	10.783	38.429
Factor 4	1.8245	7.933	46.362
Factor 5	1.7813	7.745	54.106
Factor 6	1.7028	7.403	61.51

It would take 23 Factors to account for all of the variance of the 23 variables; however the first six factors explain over 61% of the variance by themselves. Reducing the 23 variables to six factors is useful for many reasons; one reason is for graphing purposes. Graphing reduced dimensions (2 or 3) provides observable insights than are not obvious with numerous dimensions. Each of the six factors are graphed against each other and viewed in two dimensions. Another useful purpose of Factor Analysis is the unobservable elements that the factors represent. By reviewing the factor loadings, the factor can be characterized and named. These names will facilitate understanding as we discuss the factors and look at charts. It would require 15 different charts to view all six factors versus each other. Instead of looking at 15 charts, the factors will first be screened to determine which ones offer the most distinction between nations in violent

conflict and nations not in violent conflict. Figure 20 depicts six charts portraying the

factor scores versus the response (not violent conflict and violent conflict). A 99%

confidence interval (white dots and dash) is also depicted to show the difference in the

means.

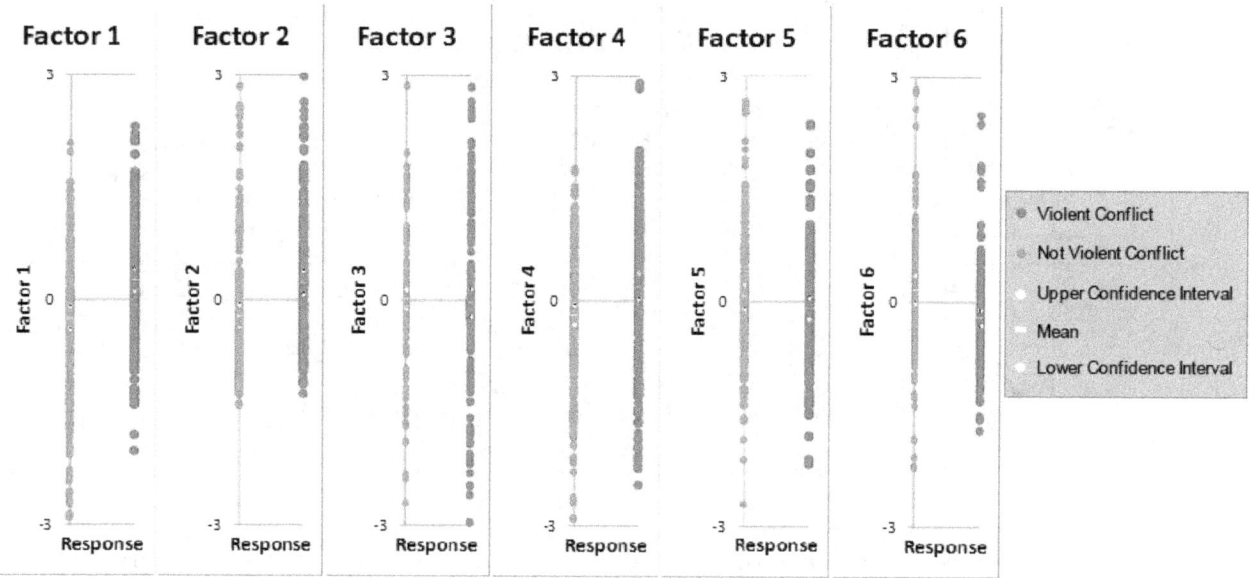

Figure 20: Factor Separation and Confidence Intervals

Factors 3 and 5 do not show adequate separation among the response, as evident in the

overlapping confidence intervals. Therefore only factors 1,2,4 and 6 will be graphed

resulting in 6 different graphs considered. All charts in Figure 20 are shown on a scale

between -3 and 3 to maintain scaling. There are outliers for factors 2, 3, 5 and 6. Some

of these outliers are analyzed next.

Recall the factor loading scores in Table 16 and the discussion concerning factor

names. Factor names are now assigned to the four selected factors in order to lend clarity to graph interpretation. Factor 1 can loosely be named "Harshness of Life" because it has high positive loadings for "Infant Mortality" and "Rural Population " as well as high negative loadings for "GDP per capita" and "Improved Water". These loadings show that factor one increases as "GDP per capita" decreases, "infant mortality" increases, "Rural Population" and "Improved Water" decreases, mimicking a "Harshness of Life" quality. Factor 2 can aptly be named "Political Oppression". This factor has high loadings scores for the variables "Freedom", "Polity IV" and "Regime Type". Political Oppression can be interpreted as increasing as the "Freedom" score increases, "Polity IV" decreases (recall that higher values are better for "Polity IV" and lower values are better for "Freedom") and "Regime Type" increases in number (Democratic = 1, Central ruler/ruling party = 2, Emerging, transitional, recent change, Disputed = 3). Factor four does not have a clear unobservable quality and will retain the name "Factor 4". Factor 6 is a combination of a nation's population density and Trade. Factor 6 increases as a nations population density and trade increase.

Figure 21 shows the four significant factors graphed against each other. Groups of clusters of primarily one type of response are numbered and circled for further analysis. The minority, or outlier responses in these groups will offer interesting insight. The factor "Trade & Population Density" has three outliers greater than 9 (2011 Singapore, 2012 Singapore, 2013 Singapore) that were not graphed. This tiny nation has extremely high population density and trade; they were excluded in order to not skew the graph.

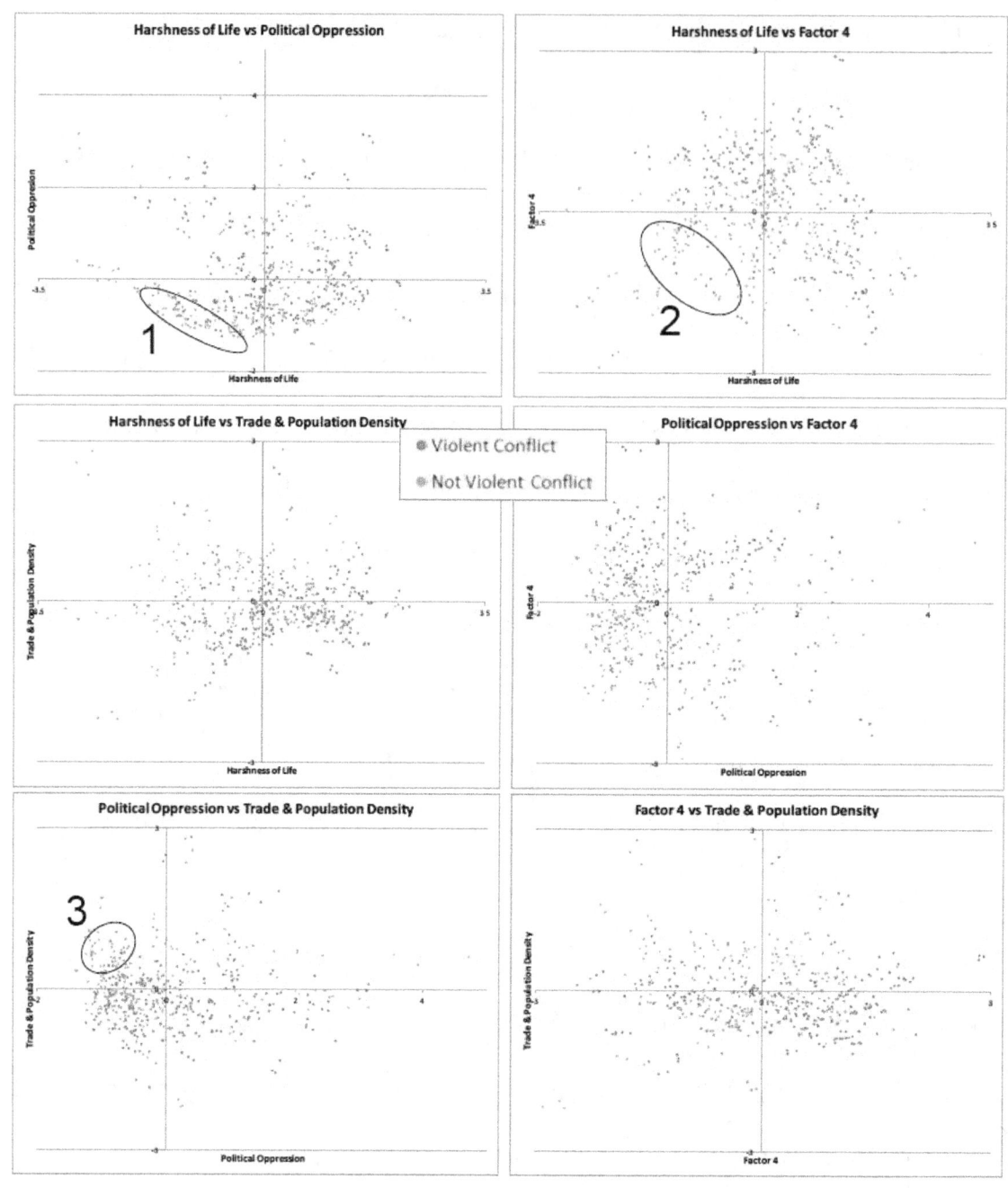

Figure 21: Graphs of Factors

Figure 22, Figure 23, and Figure 24 show the numbered and circled portions of the

graphs in Figure 21 with nations labeled for analysis.

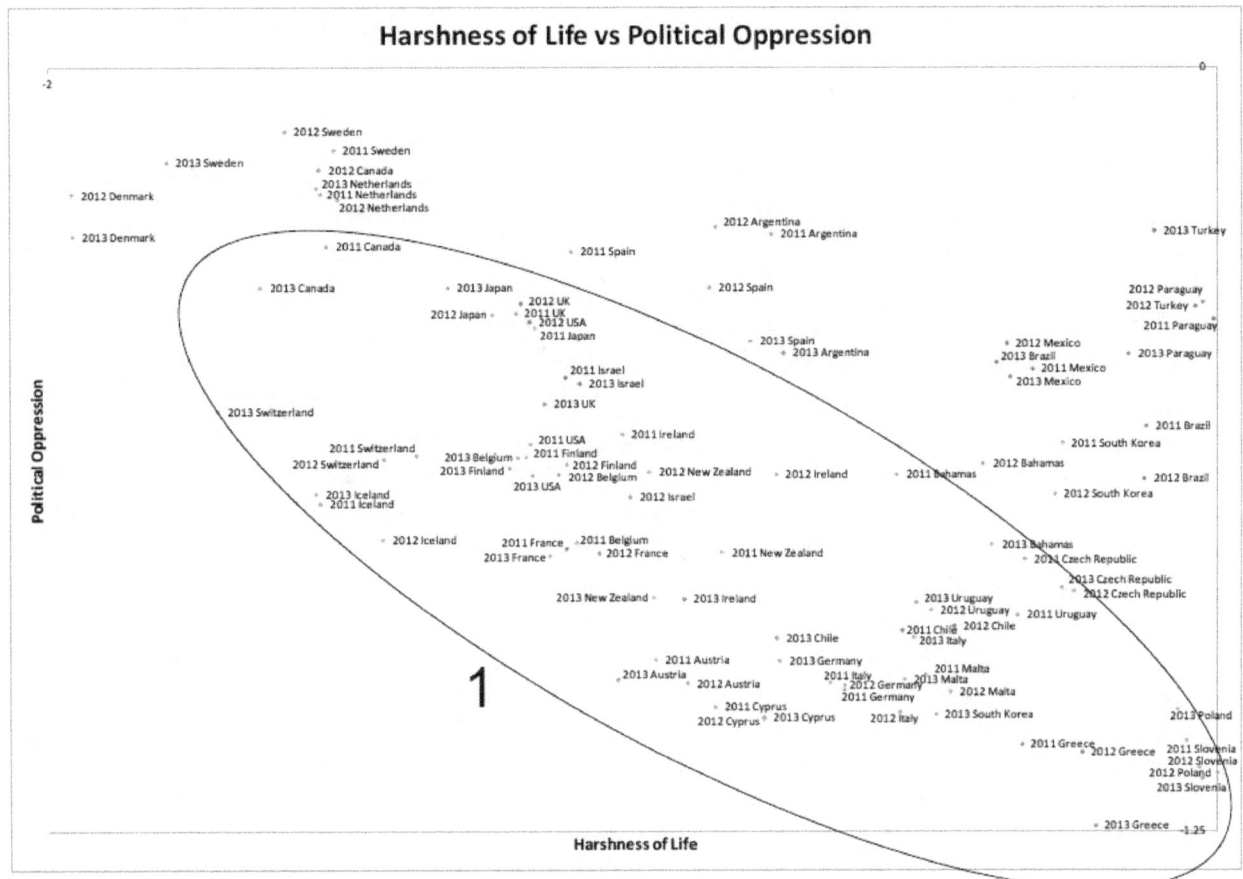

Figure 22: Harshness of Life vs Political Oppression Lower Left Quadrant

All of the circled nations in Figure 22 are considered western nations and have the

lowest political oppression and lowest harshness of life of all nations. The majority of

these nations, understandably, are not in a violent conflict. The exceptions are Israel

Greece, Chile, Ireland, France, the United Kingdom and the United States. An argument

can be raised that some of these countries, such as the United States, France, and the

United Kingdom are in a violent conflict by choice. Violent conflict is not restricted to

within a nation's border but also includes violent conflict abroad. These anomalies may introduce noise into the model. For example, all three of these countries were in a violent conflict in 2012 and all of the 9 trial models predicted they would not be in conflict. Future models could screen the database for nations that enter into conflict by choice and remove them from the dataset.

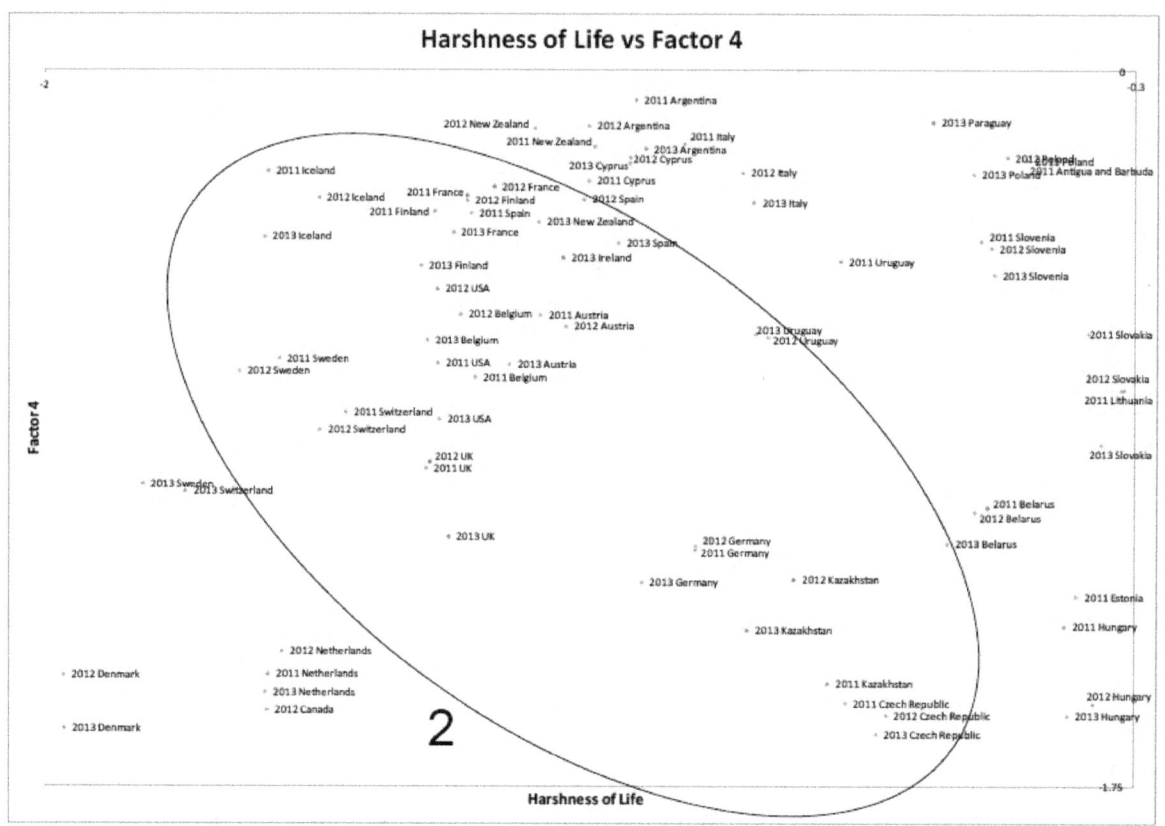

Figure 23: Harshness of Life vs Factor 4 Lower Left Quadrant

Figure 23 depicts the factors "Harshness of Life" on the x-axis and "Factor 4" on the y-axis. The nations circled in Figure 23 that are in a violent conflict also include the United States, United Kingdom and France and strengthen the argument for removing these nations from future analysis.

64

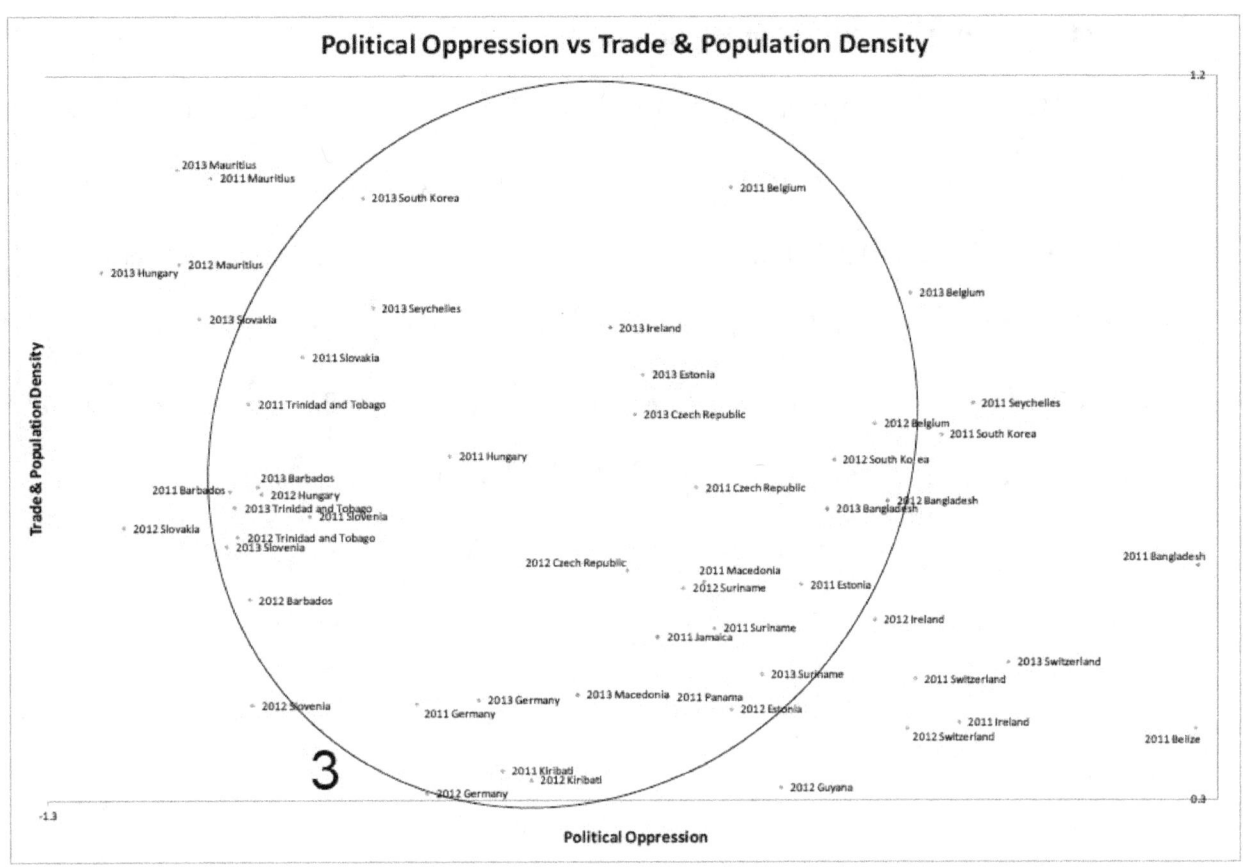

Figure 24: Political Oppression vs Trade & Population Density Upper Left Quadrant

The nations circled in Figure 24 are nations that have lower political oppression and above average trade and population density. The majority of these nations are not in a violent conflict, the exceptions include Macedonia, Panama, Jamaica, Ireland and Bangladesh. No clear conclusion is evident from these anomalies. One interesting observation from these figures are the movement of nations in this two dimensional space across time. This dynamic was examined later as a predictor of conflict and shown not to be significant.

65

Models without nations that enter into conflict by choice

Because of the insights gained from the factor analysis plots, four nation data points were removed from the model set (2011 France, 2012 France, 2012 United States, 2012 United Kingdom) and 1 data point was removed from the validation set (2013 United Kingdom). Method 3, iteratively removing the least significant variable, was used to construct two new models. Trial Model 10, shown in Figure 25, includes 9 main effect variables that are significant at an alpha = .1. Trial Model 11, also shown in Figure 25 was constructed with all main effects from Trial Model 10 and their 2nd order polynomials that are significant at an alpha = .1; hierarchy is enforced.

Trial Model 10

Whole Model Test

Model	-LogLikelihood	DF	ChiSquare	Prob>ChiSq
Difference	65.64624	9	131.2925	<.0001*
Full	182.08373			
Reduced	247.72997			

Effect Likelihood Ratio Tests

Source	Nparm	DF	L-R ChiSquare	Prob>ChiSq
2 Yr Freedom Trend	1	1	3.56571508	0.0590
Rural Pop	1	1	5.57483974	0.0182*
Death Rate	1	1	9.27565271	0.0023*
Refugees Asylum	1	1	3.10694775	0.0780
GDP per Capita	1	1	13.6616007	0.0002*
Improved Water	1	1	7.04577883	0.0079*
Trade	1	1	12.4104527	0.0004*
Freedom	1	1	24.5734874	<.0001*
Polity IV	1	1	6.8193024	0.0090*

Confusion Matrix

75.28%	Predicted 0	Predicted 1
Actual 0	149	49
Actual 1	40	122

360 nations predicted

Trial Model 11

Whole Model Test

Model	-LogLikelihood	DF	ChiSquare	Prob>ChiSq
Difference	80.38970	13	160.7794	<.0001*
Full	167.34027			
Reduced	247.72997			

Effect Likelihood Ratio Tests

Source	Nparm	DF	L-R ChiSquare	Prob>ChiSq
2 Yr Freedom Trend	1	1	4.18481279	0.0408*
Death Rate	1	1	18.1650641	<.0001*
Death Rate*Death Rate	1	1	11.4998303	0.0007*
Refugees Asylum	1	1	3.03907066	0.0813
GDP per Capita	1	1	0.42741791	0.5133
GDP per Capita*GDP per Capita	1	1	5.52074523	0.0188*
Improved Water	1	1	0.03844195	0.8446
Trade	1	1	22.6704522	<.0001*
Freedom	1	1	31.0354258	<.0001*
Freedom*Freedom	1	1	12.6372813	0.0004*
Polity IV	1	1	9.11986485	0.0025*
Polity IV*Polity IV	1	1	3.39302445	0.0655
Improved Water*Improved Water	1	1	2.77862666	0.0955

Confusion Matrix

76.67%	Predicted 0	Predicted 1
Actual 0	152	46
Actual 1	38	124

360 nations predicted

Figure 25: Trial Model 10 and Trial Model 11

The results of the prediction accuracy for the model set, validation set and combined sets is shown in Table 17. Surprisingly, the validation set prediction accuracy is lower in Trial Model 11 than in Trial Model 7. By removing the nations that enter into conflict by choice and creating a new model, six additional nations were counted as false negatives and two less nations were counted as false positives in the validation set. Removing the nations that enter into conflict by choice appears statistically insignificant. Using the validation prediction accuracy as a metric for success, Trial Model 7 continues to offer the most promising results.

Table 17: New Prediction Accuracy

Construction Method	Trial Model #	Num of Variables	Prediction Accuracy		
			Model Set	Validation Set	Model and Validation Set
Method 1 - Correlation Method	1	7	73.1%	72.0%	72.7%
	2	6	74.2%	71.4%	73.3%
	3	8	74.2%	74.2%	74.2%
Method 2 - Alternate	4	4	73.6%	73.1%	73.4%
Method 3 - Least Significant Method	5	8	74.7%	74.7%	74.7%
	6	5	74.2%	72.0%	73.4%
	7	10	75.3%	76.4%	75.6%
	8	7	76.1%	72.5%	74.9%
	9	7	73.4%	73.1%	74.9%
	10	9	75.3%	74.6%	75.0%
	11	13	76.7%	74.0%	75.8%

Initial Sensitivity Analysis

Trial Model 7 is the best model from the initial portion of analysis. Various methods are used to conduct sensitivity analysis. The next section conducts sensitivity analysis through adjusting the logistic regression cut off level. Other methods are available for sensitivity analysis but the chosen method allows for analysis on adjusting the cut off level and observing the effects on the prediction accuracy, percent of false negatives and percent of false positives as well as provides a viable option for sensitivity analysis later in this study for six sub-models.

Adjusting Logistic Regression Cut off Level for Trial Model 7

Trial Model 7 predicts the validation test set with 76.4% accuracy. If the goal is to predict which nations are in violent conflict then it is arguably better to decrease the number of times the model predicts "Not in Violent Conflict" but the nation is actually in "Violent Conflict". This error is called a false negative. The inaccurate predictions are almost evenly split between false positives (11.5%) and false negatives (12.8%). Logistic regression uses a value of .5 as a cut off for its fitted response equation. If the fitted response equation for each nation is greater than or equal to .5 then the nation is said to be in a violent conflict. Adjusting the logistic regression cut off level allows for sensitivity analysis. Figure 26 shows a graph of the prediction accuracy, false negative and false positive percents as the logistic regression cut off levels are adjusted between 0 and 1. Notice the prediction accuracy plateaus around 75% for a range of cut off levels between .35 and .5. Little change in the prediction accuracy between .35 and .5 shows a robustness of parsimonious model. Cut off levels below .35 and above .5 experiences a negative slope in prediction accuracy as they approach the extremes. The cut off level can be adjusted to .35 and the model can still attain over 75% prediction accuracy for the combined training and test set. With this cut off level the false negative prediction percent becomes 6.4% and the false positive prediction percent is 18%, satisfying the

68

desire to err on the side of false negatives. By adjusting the cut off level the percent of

nations in a violent conflict that were mis-identified is cut in half. A receiver operating

characteristic (ROC) curve would yield the same conclusions as the above analysis but

does not draw attention to the persistent errors and does not delineate the false negatives

and false positives.

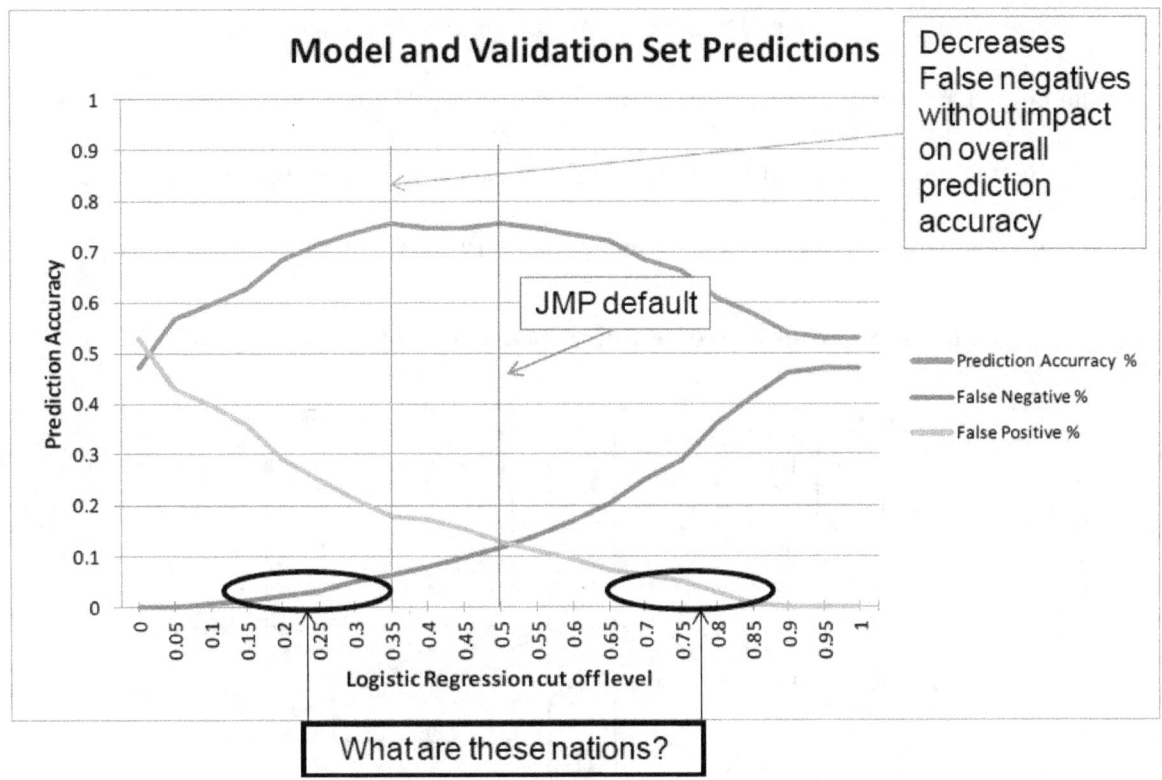

Figure 26: Confusion matrix results when adjusting the cut off value

Another aspect that warrants further investigation are the nations that continue to be false

negatives as the logistic regression cut off level approaches 0 and the nations that

continue to be false positives as the logistic regression cut off level approaches 1.

Table 18 shows a truncated list of the false negatives and false positives for both

the model set (on the left) and the validation set (on the right). Only false predictions that are greater than .15 in error, as circled in Figure 26 are shown. The lists are filtered so the most egregious errors are on the top. As expected, France, the United Kingdom and the United States are near the top of the false negative list. Nations in the validation set that were also false predictions in the model set are highlighted in yellow. With regard to the model set, 21 of the 41 false negatives are greater than .15 in error and 27 of the 49 false positives are greater than .15 in error. With regard to the validation set, 14 of the 22 false negatives are greater than .15 in error and 13 of the 21 false positives are greater than .15 in error. The nations near the top of the false positive list appear, according to the model, destined for conflict. This concept is analyzed further later.

Table 18: List of Extreme False Positives and False Negatives

Trial Model 7 Model set False Predictions				
False Negatives	**Prob**	**False Positives**	**Prob**
2011 France	0.085864	2012 Oman	0.86167
2012 France	0.104179	2011 West Bank and Gaza	0.84828
2012 United States of America	0.10586	2011 Brunei Darussalam	0.844397
2012 United Kingdom	0.113298	2012 West Bank and Gaza	0.84106
2011 Panama	0.125798	2012 Eritrea	0.838545
2012 Panama	0.151104	2011 Guinea Bissau	0.831302
2012 Belize	0.184803	2012 Madagascar	0.827212
2011 Chile	0.215141	2012 Brunei Darussalam	0.818429
2011 Greece	0.236876	2011 Chad	0.815074
2011 Belarus	0.239984	2012 Solomon Islands	0.797931
2012 Serbia	0.247116	2012 Haiti	0.796887
2011 Bosnia and Herzegovina	0.264756	2011 Eritrea	0.796583
2012 Chile	0.27345	2012 Cuba	0.791147
2012 Samoa	0.285518	2011 Solomon Islands	0.789735
2011 Serbia	0.297989	2012 Uzbekistan	0.764547
2012 Greece	0.298022	2011 Cuba	0.750406
2011 South Africa	0.302231	2011 Armenia	0.743739
2012 Romania	0.304865	2012 Tonga	0.74365
2011 Jamaica	0.308543	2012 Cameroon	0.73726
2012 Maldives	0.329568	2012 Mozambique	0.734566
2011 Thailand	0.332851	2012 Zambia	0.718343
		2012 Sri Lanka	0.715278
		2011 Venezuela	0.702026
		2011 Uzbekistan	0.694431
		2012 United Arab Emirates	0.68165
		2011 Ecuador	0.668797
		2011 United Arab Emirates	0.66083
*2012 Macedonia	0.377555	*2011 Gabon	0.518288
*2012 Viet Nam	0.388843		

Trial Model 7 Validation set False Predictions				
False Negatives	**Prob**	**False Positives**	**Prob**
2013 Ireland	0.007819	2013 Madagascar	0.895929
2013 United Kingdom	0.093389	2013 West Bank and Gaza	0.862994
2013 Bulgaria	0.148941	2013 Sierra Leone	0.862368
2013 Panama	0.151442	2013 Eritrea	0.848904
2013 Belize	0.162745	2013 Oman	0.848883
2013 Serbia	0.211048	2013 Côte D'Ivoire	0.811245
2013 Ukraine	0.245703	2013 Guinea Bissau	0.806115
2013 Chile	0.263432	2013 Solomon Islands	0.798932
2013 Romania	0.274939	2013 Uzbekistan	0.79779
2013 Maldives	0.278364	2013 Laos	0.772463
2013 Republic of Moldova	0.281728	2013 Cuba	0.764878
2013 Viet Nam	0.309773	2013 Gabon	0.690189
2013 Greece	0.312793	2013 Zambia	0.652305
2013 Macedonia	0.328002		

⟹ - Nations that were identified as in a violent conflict by choice

* - False predictions that are not greater than .15 in error in the model set but are greater than .15 in error in the validation set

Many of the false negatives are Western and Latin American nations and many of the false positives are African nations. These observations identify a potential need for a variable to explain a nation's region.   The green arrows in Table 18 identify outlier nations that are potentially in conflict by choice. These nations were discussed in the section "Factor Analysis and Noise Reduction techniques". Simply deleting these false negatives from the confusion matrix results yields 76.1% prediction accuracy for the model set and 76.8% accuracy for the validation set, as shown in Figure 27. This is an increase from 75.3% and 76.4%. Note the yellow and blue shaded confusion matrices in Figure 27; in this study yellow shaded confusion matrices indicate the model set while blue shaded confusion matrices indicate the validation set.

Trial Model 7 Model Set				Trial Model 7 Validation Set			
76.11%		Predicted		**76.80%**		Predicted	
		0	1			0	1
Actual	0	149	49	Actual	0	70	21
	1	37	125		1	21	69
360 rows of data				181 rows of data			

Figure 27: Confusion Matrices Excluding Nations in Conflict by Choice

Analysis using an expanded database

The database was initially constrained by available data for a few variables; "The HIIK Trend" variable and the "Border Conflict" variable. Each of these variables is calculated using dependent variable scores with a two or three year lag. Neither of these variables has proven significant and will now be removed from consideration. Without these variables the database can expand to five years, instead of three, because the remaining variables have complete data back through 1973 (or 2001 for Caloric Intake) and the database is now only constrained by availability of the dependent variable. Three years (2009, 2010, and 2011) are used to construct the model and 2 years (2012 and

2013) are used to validate. This split allows 546 rows of nations for building the model and 346 rows of nations for validating the model, providing a sufficiently large dataset for model building and validation. An expanded database becomes essential later when models for each region are constructed. The previous data set did not have enough data points to properly construct 6 "sub models".

Trial Model 7 is first applied to the expanded database. A breakout of prediction accuracy by region will prove useful for the next portion of analysis. A breakout for Trial Model 7 is shown in Figure 28. While results are shown by region, so far no explicit variable accounts for differing regions within the model.

Trial Model 7 applied to expanded database

Sub Saharan Africa

Sub Saharan Africa - Model Set

70.07%	Predicted 0	Predicted 1
Actual 0	46	32
Actual 1	12	57

147 rows of data

Sub Saharan Africa - Validation Set

71.43%	Predicted 0	Predicted 1
Actual 0	26	22
Actual 1	6	44

98 rows of data

South & East Asia

South & East Asia - Model Set

70.24%	Predicted 0	Predicted 1
Actual 0	32	16
Actual 1	9	27

84 rows of data

South & East Asia - Validation Set

69.64%	Predicted 0	Predicted 1
Actual 0	18	7
Actual 1	10	21

56 rows of data

E. Europe & C. Asia

E. Europe & C. Asia - Model Set

75.00%	Predicted 0	Predicted 1
Actual 0	41	10
Actual 1	11	22

84 rows of data

E. Europe & C. Asia - Validation Set

71.43%	Predicted 0	Predicted 1
Actual 0	21	6
Actual 1	10	19

56 rows of data

OECD - Organization for Economic Co-operation and Development

Arab Countries

Arab Countries - Model Set

68.63%	Predicted 0	Predicted 1
Actual 0	7	14
Actual 1	2	28

51 rows of data

Arab Countries - Validation Set

76.47%	Predicted 0	Predicted 1
Actual 0	2	6
Actual 1	2	24

34 rows of data

OECD

OECD - Model Set

81.82%	Predicted 0	Predicted 1
Actual 0	75	0
Actual 1	18	6

99 rows of data

OECD - Validation Set

83.33%	Predicted 0	Predicted 1
Actual 0	51	0
Actual 1	11	4

66 rows of data

Latin America

Latin America - Model Set

83.95%	Predicted 0	Predicted 1
Actual 0	43	8
Actual 1	5	25

81 rows of data

Latin America - Validation Set

81.48%	Predicted 0	Predicted 1
Actual 0	20	4
Actual 1	6	24

54 rows of data

World prediction accuracies

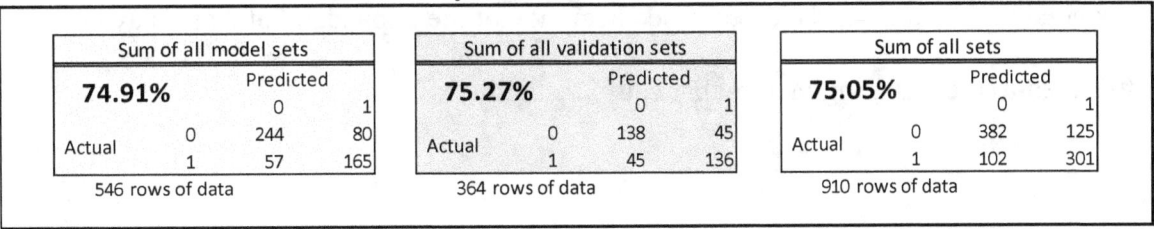

Sum of all model sets

74.91%	Predicted 0	Predicted 1
Actual 0	244	80
Actual 1	57	165

546 rows of data

Sum of all validation sets

75.27%	Predicted 0	Predicted 1
Actual 0	138	45
Actual 1	45	136

364 rows of data

Sum of all sets

75.05%	Predicted 0	Predicted 1
Actual 0	382	125
Actual 1	102	301

910 rows of data

Figure 28: Trial Model 7 Applied to Expanded Database

When TM 7 is applied to the expanded database it has similar accuracy to the smaller database. The break out of prediction accuracies by region shows inconsistencies that identify a need for another variable for geographic region. Additionally, TM 7 was constructed off of data from 2011-2012. With the expanded database TM 7 is validated using 2012-2013 data. Because of this overlapping model building and validation set it is necessary to construct a new model for the expanded database.

As done previously with the 2011-2013 smaller database used to develop Trial Model 7, the "Least Significant method" is used to construct a new model with the 2009-2013 larger database, Trial Model 12. The results are shown in Figure 29 (confusion matrix shown in Figure 30, broken out by region). As with Trial Model 7, an alpha = .1 is used and 2nd order polynomials from the three most significant main effects are tested for inclusion. Trial model 12 differs from Trial Model 7 in a number of ways. Some variables are included in Trial Model 12 that were in not Trial Model 7. Specifically "3 Yr Freedom Trend", "5 Yr Freedom Trend", "Population densities", "Rural Population", "Infant Mortality" and "Regime Type" are included. Some variables are not included in Trial Model 12 that were in Trial Model 7. Specifically, the variables "2 yr Freedom Trend", "Death Rate"," Death Rate *Death Rate" and "GDP per Capita*GDP per Capita" were not included. The validation set prediction accuracy overall decreases with the expanded validation set. This decreased accuracy of the expanded database may be attributed to the changing factors that cause instability over time.

Trial Model 12

Whole Model Test

Model	-LogLikelihood	DF	ChiSquare	Prob>ChiSq
Difference	105.56361	13	211.1272	<.0001*
Full	263.31107			
Reduced	368.87468			

Effect Likelihood Ratio Tests

Source	Nparm	DF	L-R ChiSquare	Prob>ChiSq
3 Yr Freedom Trend	1	1	5.9881414	0.0144*
5 yr Freedom Trend	1	1	6.40282367	0.0114*
Pop density	1	1	10.1749571	0.0014*
Rural Pop	1	1	10.2611648	0.0014*
GDP per Capita	1	1	7.55044987	0.0060*
Infant Mortality	1	1	4.36881024	0.0366*
Improved Water	1	1	17.5541153	<.0001*
Trade	1	1	51.9544803	<.0001*
Freedom	1	1	51.7094704	<.0001*
Polity IV	1	1	21.336675	<.0001*
Regime Type	2	2	9.60874057	0.0082*
Religious Diversity	1	1	9.15909335	0.0025*

Figure 29: Expanded Database

Regional confusion matrices for Trial Model 12 are shown in Figure 30. Note the inconsistent prediction accuracies among the regions. These inconsistencies suggest the need for another variable. For this reason, a "Region" variable is introduced into the model.

Trial Model 12

Sub Saharan Africa

Sub Saharan Africa - Model Set			
76.19%		Predicted	
		0	1
Actual	0	56	22
	1	13	56

147 rows of data

Sub Saharan Africa - Validation Set			
65.31%		Predicted	
		0	1
Actual	0	29	19
	1	15	35

98 rows of data

South & East Asia

South & East Asia - Model Set			
85.71%		Predicted	
		0	1
Actual	0	40	8
	1	4	32

84 rows of data

South & East Asia - Validation Set			
62.50%		Predicted	
		0	1
Actual	0	15	10
	1	11	20

56 rows of data

E. Europe & C. Asia

E. Europe & C. Asia - Model Set			
78.57%		Predicted	
		0	1
Actual	0	42	9
	1	9	24

84 rows of data

E. Europe & C. Asia - Validation Set			
67.86%		Predicted	
		0	1
Actual	0	21	6
	1	12	17

56 rows of data

Arab Countries

Arab Countries - Model Set			
74.51%		Predicted	
		0	1
Actual	0	16	5
	1	8	22

51 rows of data

Arab Countries - Validation Set			
73.53%		Predicted	
		0	1
Actual	0	5	3
	1	6	20

34 rows of data

OECD

OECD - Model Set			
83.84%		Predicted	
		0	1
Actual	0	70	5
	1	11	13

99 rows of data

OECD - Validation Set			
84.85%		Predicted	
		0	1
Actual	0	46	5
	1	5	10

66 rows of data

Latin America

Latin America - Model Set			
76.54%		Predicted	
		0	1
Actual	0	39	12
	1	7	23

81 rows of data

Latin America - Validation Set			
77.78%		Predicted	
		0	1
Actual	0	20	4
	1	8	22

54 rows of data

Sum of all model sets			
79.30%		Predicted	
		0	1
Actual	0	263	61
	1	52	170

546 rows of data

Sum of all validation sets			
71.43%		Predicted	
		0	1
Actual	0	136	47
	1	57	124

364 rows of data

Sum of all sets			
76.15%		Predicted	
		0	1
Actual	0	399	108
	1	109	294

910 rows of data

Figure 30: Trial Model 12 by Regions

Addition of variable "Region"

A new variable "Region" is introduced in an effort to improve the model. Five different groupings of nations into regions are explored. These five different groupings are shown in Figure 31.

Region 1			Region 2			Region 3			Region 4			Region 5	
Africa	54		Africa	53		Africa	54		Africa	53		Arab Countries	17
Asia	45		Asia	40		Asia	54		Asia	39		Eastern Europe and Central Asia	28
Europe	42		Europe	41		Europe	43		Europe	42		Latin America	27
Oceania	10		Middle East	17		Americas	31		Middle East	17		OECD	33
North America	19		North America	19					Americas	31		South and East Asia	28
South America	12		South America	12								Sub Saharan Africa	49

Figure 31: Region Groups

Each of these five region groupings were tested for inclusion as a nominal variable using the least significant method. "Region 5" proved the best of the groupings and was renamed "Region" for the duration of the study. This particular grouping was inspired by a 2006 Hans Rosling video (The best stats you've ever seen, 2006). The model with this new nominal variable is named Trial Model 13 and results are shown in Figure 32. The validation set prediction accuracy increases from Trial Model 12, confirming the inclusion of a "Region" variable.

77

Trial Model 13

Whole Model Test

Model	-LogLikelihood	DF	ChiSquare	Prob>ChiSq
Difference	128.79673	20	257.5935	<.0001*
Full	240.07795			
Reduced	368.87468			

Effect Likelihood Ratio Tests

Source	Nparm	DF	L-R ChiSquare	Prob>ChiSq
Region	5	5	48.2153011	<.0001*
3 Yr Freedom Trend	1	1	7.80349508	0.0052*
5 yr Freedom Trend	1	1	7.38654104	0.0066*
Pop density	1	1	4.60270232	0.0319*
Rural Pop	1	1	6.19023737	0.0128*
Refugees Asylum	1	1	5.20904688	0.0225*
GDP per Capita	1	1	15.8153742	<.0001*
Improved Water	1	1	18.3581712	<.0001*
Unemployment	1	1	4.99213049	0.0255*
Trade	1	1	35.8330412	<.0001*
Caloric intake	1	1	4.46570445	0.0346*
Freedom	1	1	59.4674642	<.0001*
Polity IV	1	1	16.0759964	<.0001*
Regime Type	2	2	5.47330349	0.0648
Freedom*Freedom	1	1	15.8781581	<.0001*

Figure 32: Model with Region Variable

A region break out of confusion matrices for Trial Model 13 is shown in Figure 33.

Overall the prediction accuracy increases by over 3 % from TM 12 and the prediction

accuracies for all regions, except for Latin America, increase. The disparities among the

region's prediction accuracies indicate that separate models for each grouping may prove

useful and are justified.

Trial Model 13

Sub Saharan Africa

Sub Saharan Africa - Model Set			
74.15%		Predicted	
		0	1
Actual	0	58	20
	1	18	51

147 rows of data

Sub Saharan Africa - Validation Set			
67.35%		Predicted	
		0	1
Actual	0	34	14
	1	18	32

98 rows of data

South & East Asia

South & East Asia - Model Set			
82.14%		Predicted	
		0	1
Actual	0	40	8
	1	7	29

84 rows of data

South & East Asia - Validation Set			
71.43%		Predicted	
		0	1
Actual	0	19	6
	1	10	21

56 rows of data

E. Europe & C. Asia

E. Europe & C. Asia - Model Set			
75.00%		Predicted	
		0	1
Actual	0	41	10
	1	11	22

84 rows of data

E. Europe & C. Asia - Validation Set			
75.00%		Predicted	
		0	1
Actual	0	23	4
	1	10	19

56 rows of data

Arab Countries

Arab Countries - Model Set			
82.35%		Predicted	
		0	1
Actual	0	16	5
	1	4	26

51 rows of data

Arab Countries - Validation Set			
79.41%		Predicted	
		0	1
Actual	0	8	3
	1	4	19

34 rows of data

OECD

OECD - Model Set			
83.84%		Predicted	
		0	1
Actual	0	70	5
	1	11	13

99 rows of data

OECD - Validation Set			
86.36%		Predicted	
		0	1
Actual	0	47	4
	1	5	10

66 rows of data

Latin America

Latin America - Model Set			
83.95%		Predicted	
		0	1
Actual	0	45	6
	1	7	23

81 rows of data

Latin America - Validation Set			
74.07%		Predicted	
		0	1
Actual	0	21	3
	1	11	19

54 rows of data

Sum of all model sets			
79.49%		Predicted	
		0	1
Actual	0	270	54
	1	58	164

546 rows of data

Sum of all validation sets			
74.73%		Predicted	
		0	1
Actual	0	152	34
	1	58	120

364 rows of data

Sum of all sets			
77.58%		Predicted	
		0	1
Actual	0	422	88
	1	116	284

910 rows of data

Figure 33: Trial Model 13 by Region

Separate Models for Six Regions

Using the region groupings from Trial Model 13, six different sub-models were constructed (Sub Sahara Africa, South & East Asia, East Europe & Central Asia, Arab, OECD and Latin America). These models were all constructed using Method two, the Alternate Correlation Method. The number of data points for some of the six sub-models was not large enough to facilitate use of the Method 3, Least Significant Method, for some sub-models so Method 2 was used for all sub-models. The sub-models, collectively called Trial Model 14, are shown in Figure 34.

Trial Model 14

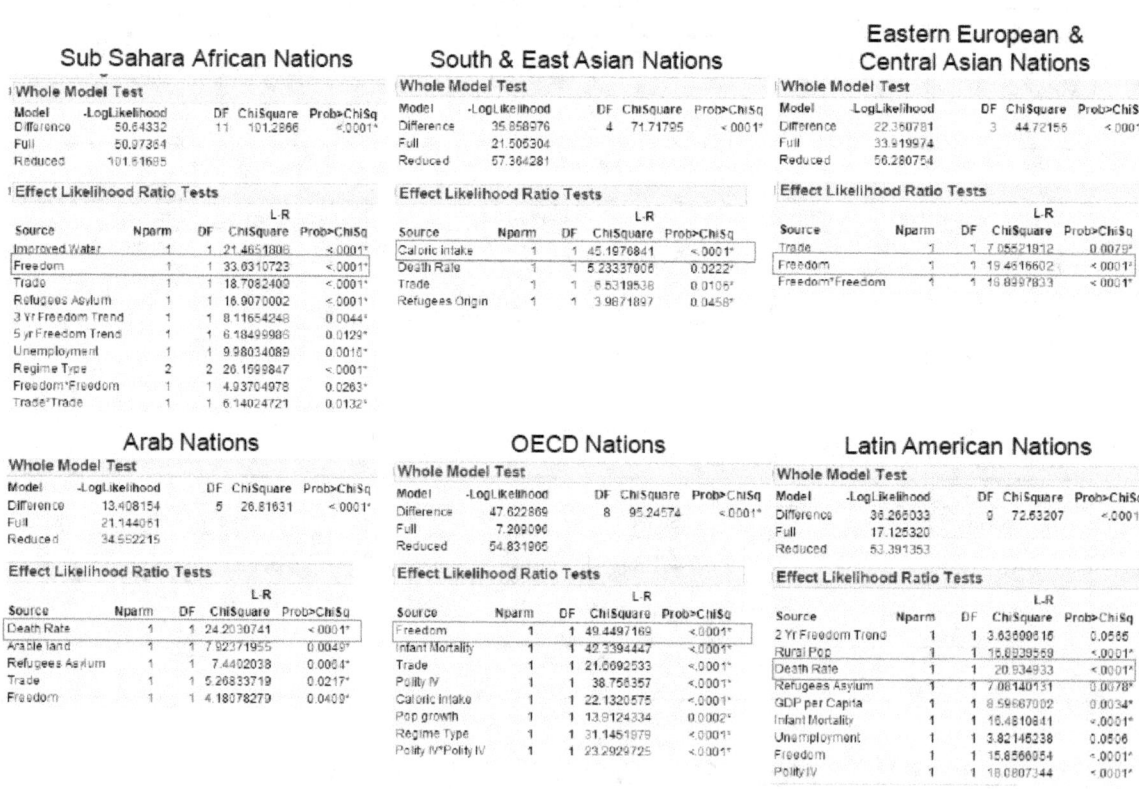

Figure 34: Trial Model 14 - Separate Region Models

Each model is distinctly different. Recall the importance of the variable "Freedom" in previous models. The variable "Freedom" remains the most significant variable for three of the six regions; Sub Sahara Africa, Eastern Europe & Central Asia and OECD. The death rate is the most important variable for Arab and Latin American nations and caloric intake is the most important variable for South and East Asian nations. The most significant variable for each sub-model is outlined in a red box. Trial Model 14 coefficients are shown in Table 19 and Trial Model 14 prediction accuracies are shown in Figure 35.

Table 19: Trial Model 14 Coefficients

Trial Model 14 Coefficients

Sub Sahara Africa

β_0 Intercept	β_1 Freedom	β_2 Improved Water	β_3 Refugees Asylum	β_4 Trade	β_5 Unemploy ment	β_6 3 yr Freedom trend	β_7 Regime Type (Central)	β_8 5 yr Freedom trend	β_9 Regime Type (Democratic)	β_{10} (Freedom-4.260)^2	β_{11} (Trade-81.378)^2
-1.7953	-1.4348	0.0968	225.1838	0.0605	-0.1902	-21.9044	-3.8044	25.9772	-2.3227	-0 3812	0.0007

South and East Asia

β_0 Intercept	β_1 Caloric Intake	β_2 Trade	β_3 Death Rate	β_3 Refugees Origin
7.6562	-0.0074	0.0308	-0.7144	410.4347

Eastern Europe and Central Asia

β_0 Intercept	β_1 Freedom	β_2 Trade	β_3 (Freedom-3.732)^2
0.1178	-0.9909	0.0298	0.4909

Arab Nations

β_0 Intercept	β_1 Death Rate	β_2 Arable Land	β_3 Refugees Asylum	β_4 Trade	β_5 Freedom
7.6700	10.6300	5.9100	5.5500	4.3000	3 8000

OECD

β_0 Intercept	β_1 Freedom	β_2 Infant Mortality	β_3 Polity IV	β_4 Regime Type (Central)	β_5 Caloric Intake	β_6 Trade	β_7 Pop Growth	β_8 (Polity IV-9.623)^2
-407 5271	-85 9598	-11.6192	54.6875	-15.3109	0 0476	0 2285	-5.1221	27.8649

Latin America

β_0 Intercept	β_1 Death Rate	β_2 Polity IV	β_3 Rural Pop	β_4 Infant Mortality	β_5 Freedom	β_6 GDP per Capita	β_7 Refugee Asylum	β_8 Unemploy ment	β_9 2 Yr Freedom Trend
1.0143	2.4126	-1.2698	0.2121	-0.2360	-3.0708	0 0006	-211.1903	-0.2993	32.0956

Trial Model 14 - Six Individual Models

Sub Saharan Africa

Sub Saharan Africa - Model Set		Predicted	
82.31%		0	1
Actual	0	64	14
	1	12	57

147 rows of data

Sub Saharan Africa - Validation Set		Predicted	
74.49%		0	1
Actual	0	39	9
	1	16	34

98 rows of data

South & East Asia

South & East Asia - Model Set		Predicted	
90.48%		0	1
Actual	0	44	4
	1	4	32

84 rows of data

South & East Asia - Validation Set		Predicted	
76.79%		0	1
Actual	0	21	4
	1	9	22

56 rows of data

E. Europe & C. Asia

E. Europe & C. Asia - Model Set		Predicted	
77.38%		0	1
Actual	0	42	9
	1	10	23

84 rows of data

E. Europe & C. Asia - Validation Set		Predicted	
75.00%		0	1
Actual	0	22	5
	1	9	20

56 rows of data

Arab Countries

Arab Countries - Model Set		Predicted	
84.31%		0	1
Actual	0	16	5
	1	3	27

51 rows of data

Arab Countries - Validation Set		Predicted	
70.59%		0	1
Actual	0	6	2
	1	8	18

34 rows of data

OECD

OECD - Model Set		Predicted	
95.96%		0	1
Actual	0	73	2
	1	2	22

99 rows of data

OECD - Validation Set		Predicted	
92.42%		0	1
Actual	0	50	1
	1	4	11

66 rows of data

Latin America

Latin America - Model Set		Predicted	
90.12%		0	1
Actual	0	47	4
	1	4	26

81 rows of data

Latin America - Validation Set		Predicted	
77.78%		0	1
Actual	0	23	1
	1	11	19

54 rows of data

Sum of all model sets		Predicted	
86.63%		0	1
Actual	0	286	38
	1	35	187

546 rows of data

Sum of all validation sets		Predicted	
78.30%		0	1
Actual	0	161	22
	1	57	124

364 rows of data

Sum of all sets		Predicted	
83.30%		0	1
Actual	0	447	60
	1	92	311

910 rows of data

Figure 35: Individual Models

The separate models show improvement for every validation set category except the Arab countries (with a lower prediction accuracy) and East Europe & Central Asia (with no change to prediction accuracy). The most notable increases are in OECD, Sub Saharan Africa and South & East Asia.

Sensitivity Analysis on the study's best model

Recall the section titled "Adjusting Logistic Regression Cut Off Level". In that portion of analysis the confusion matrix results for Trial Model 7 were calculated and graphed for different cut off values ranging from 0 to 1. This same analysis is conducted for Trial Model 14. The goal is to test the robustness of the cut off level. Two graphs are shown in Figure 36; on the left is the prediction accuracies from the model set (2009-2011) and the graph on the right shows the prediction accuracies from the validation set (2012-2013).

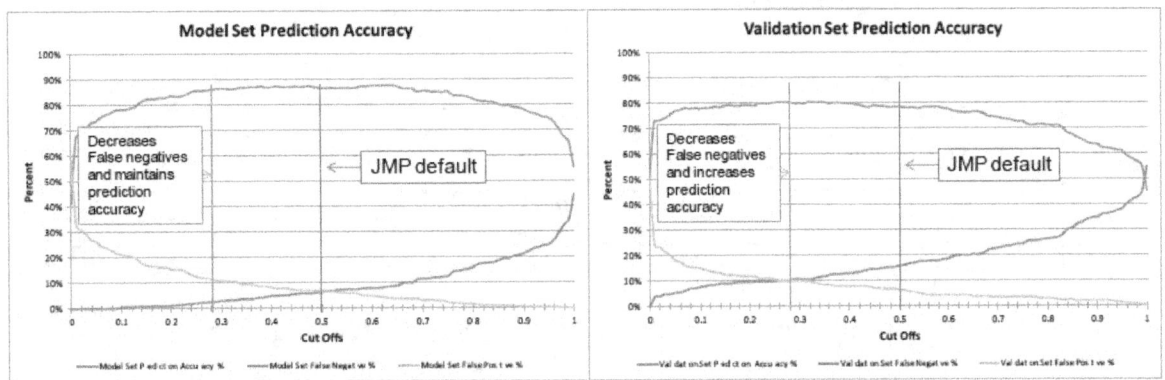

Figure 36: Prediction Accuracies

The default cut off value is 0.5. When the default value is used the model set prediction accuracy is 86.6% and the model set false predictions are fairly evenly split between false negatives (6.4%) and false positives (7%). As previously argued, it is better to predict a false negative than a false positive. With the default "cut off value", the

Trial Model 14 predicts a balanced number of false negatives and false positives for the model set, but when the same model is applied to the validation set, the model predicted more than twice as many false negatives (15.7%) as false positives (6%). This is undesirable if the goal is to minimize the false negatives. The Model set maintains a prediction accuracy above 85% for all cut off values between 0.25 and 0.69. In this same interval the validation set maintains prediction accuracies above 74%. This "plateau" of prediction accuracies allows for a deviation in cut off values.

Different Levels of false negative percents are analyzed. Table 20 shows results when the false negative percent is less than 5% and when the false negative percent is less than 2.5%. The cut off level is 0.41 when the model set false negative percent is less than 5% and 0.27 when the model set false negative percent is less than 2.5%.

Table 20: False Positives at 5% and 2.5%

Cut Off Value	Model Set (2009-2011)			Validation Set (2012-2013)		
	Model Set False Negative %	Model Set False Positive %	Model Set Prediction Accuracy %	Validation Set False Negative %	Validation Set False Positive %	Validation Set Prediction Accuracy %
0.41	4.95%	7.88%	87.18%	12.91%	7.69%	79.40%
0.27	2.38%	11.90%	85.71%	9.89%	9.89%	80.22%
0.28	2.56%	11.54%	85.90%	9.89%	9.89%	80.22%

For a 0.28 cut off level (green arrow), the model set false negative percent is nearly 2.5% and it has equal or better results than the model with a cut off of 0.27. Adjusting the cutoff value to 0.28 yields 80.22% prediction accuracy for the validation set and an equal amount of false positives (36) and false negatives (36). This new model, with the new cut off of 0.28, becomes Trial Model 14a and is the study's best model, as measured by validation set prediction accuracy. Predictions accuracies for the regions for Trial Model 14a are shown in Figure 37.

84

Trial Model 14a - Six Individual Models with cutoff of .28

Sub Saharan Africa

Sub Saharan Africa - Model Set		
82.31%	Predicted	
	0	1
Actual 0	56	22
1	4	65

147 rows of data

Sub Saharan Africa - Validation Set		
77.55%	Predicted	
	0	1
Actual 0	33	15
1	7	43

98 rows of data

South & East Asia

South & East Asia - Model Set		
90.48%	Predicted	
	0	1
Actual 0	41	7
1	1	35

84 rows of data

South & East Asia - Validation Set		
80.36%	Predicted	
	0	1
Actual 0	21	4
1	7	24

56 rows of data

E. Europe & C. Asia

E. Europe & C. Asia - Model Set		
78.57%	Predicted	
	0	1
Actual 0	36	15
1	3	30

84 rows of data

E. Europe & C. Asia - Validation Set		
71.43%	Predicted	
	0	1
Actual 0	17	10
1	6	23

56 rows of data

Arab Countries

Arab Countries - Model Set		
78.43%	Predicted	
	0	1
Actual 0	12	9
1	2	28

51 rows of data

Arab Countries - Validation Set		
82.35%	Predicted	
	0	1
Actual 0	4	4
1	2	24

34 rows of data

OECD

OECD - Model Set		
94.95%	Predicted	
	0	1
Actual 0	71	4
1	1	23

99 rows of data

OECD - Validation Set		
92.42%	Predicted	
	0	1
Actual 0	50	1
1	4	11

66 rows of data

Latin America

Latin America - Model Set		
88.89%	Predicted	
	0	1
Actual 0	45	6
1	3	27

81 rows of data

Latin America - Validation Set		
77.78%	Predicted	
	0	1
Actual 0	22	2
1	10	20

54 rows of data

Sum of all model sets		
85.90%	Predicted	
	0	1
Actual 0	261	63
1	14	208

546 rows of data

Sum of all validation sets		
80.22%	Predicted	
	0	1
Actual 0	147	36
1	36	145

364 rows of data

Sum of all sets		
83.63%	Predicted	
	0	1
Actual 0	408	99
1	50	353

910 rows of data

Figure 37: Trial Model 14, Cutoff of .28

Trial Model 14a shows an overall validation set prediction accuracy improvement from Trial Model 14 of almost 2%. Three of the sub-models (Sub Sahara Africa, South and East Asia, and Arab Countries) show improved accuracy; two of the sub-models (OECD

85

and Latin America) show no change; and the accuracy of predictions for Eastern Europe and Central Asia decreases.

Methods to Predict Nations not currently in Violent Conflict transitioning to Violent Conflict

Next, the study explores only those nations that transition from a state of "not in violent conflict" to "violent conflict". Two methods are explored and presented. The first method did not prove successful but is presented to further the discussion in this area. The second method offered useful insights.

Method 1 – Logistic Regression using several previous year's data

Another database was compiled of new nations to a violent conflict and years previous that were in a state of "Not violent conflict". Only nations with a period of "not violence" for at least 2 consecutive years before the transition to violence were included. The goal was to have a distinct period of "not violent conflict" years and then the "violent conflict" year. The alternate correlation method was used to construct a model and test for variable significance. Only one variable was significant for this data. The variable "3 year freedom trend" was significant at an alpha = 0.09 but the results were not useable. The model predicted 168 of the 169 nations to be in a state of "not violence" and predicted only one nation (2013 Ukraine) to be in a state of "violent conflict". Therefore, the model is not a useful predictor of nations in violent conflict. Figure 38 shows the confusion matrix results.

Method 2 - Complete set			
75.15%		Predicted	
		0	1
Actual	0	126	0
	1	42	1

169 rows of data

Figure 38: Method 2 Confusion Matrix

Method 2 – Markov chain muli-year model using Trial Model 14

A second method was investigated to identify new nations to conflict. This method assumes independence between years and assumes the conditions do not change substantially between years. Using Trial Model 14, there are 60 false negatives from 2009 - 2013. Analyzing these false negatives and how they behave the following year will lend insight into nations entering conflict. First the mathematical likelihoods for these false negatives are explored. A nation that is falsely predicted to be in conflict (at probability = 0.5) has the probabilities shown in Table 21 for the following four years. This table also shows the mathematical likelihood for nations with a probability equal to 0.75 for the following four years, assuming independence. Note that the mathematical likelihood are strictly for nations with a probability equal to 0.5 and equal to 0.75 while the historical probabilities are for 0.5 and higher and for 0.75 and higher.

Table 21: Mathematical Likelihood of False Negatives

Mathematical Probability of False Negatives entering Violent Conflict in 1-4 years				
Nations with a prob of .5				
	Violent Conflict within 1 yr	Violent Conflict within 2 yrs	Violent Conflict within 3 yrs	Violent Conflict within 4 yrs
Probability	50.0%	75.0%	87.5%	93.75%
Nations with a prob of .75				
Probability	75.0%	93.75%	98.44%	99.61%

The historical probabilities from this study are analyzed next. The 15 false negatives from 2009 are analyzed for violent conflict within 1 yr, within 2 years, within 3 years and within 4 years. The 9 false negatives from 2010 are analyzed for violent conflict with 1 year, within 2 years, and within 3 years. The 14 false negatives from 2011 are analyzed for violent conflict with 1 year and within 2 years. The 11 false negatives from 2012 are analyzed for violent conflict with 1 year. As of this analysis there is no HIIK data for 2014 so the 12 false negatives for 2013 cannot be analyzed. Table 22 shows the analysis results. According to the years analyzed, a nation incorrectly predicted to be in a violent conflict but is actually not in violent conflict enters into a violent conflict the following year 29 out of 49 times, or 59.2% of the time. Thirty out of 38 nations (78.9%) nations entered a violent conflict within the next two years, 22 out of 25 (88%) enter a violent conflict within the next 3 years and a 14 out of 15 (93.3%) enter a violent conflict within the next 4 years. The historical data closely follows the expected mathematical likelihood.

Table 22: Historical probability of False Negatives

**Historical Probability of
False Negatives entering Violent Conflict in 1-4 years**

	Violent Conflict within 1 yr	Violent Conflict within 2 yrs	Violent Conflict within 3 yrs	Violent Conflict within 4 yrs
Nations with a prob of .5 or higher				
Probability	59.2%	78.9%	88.0%	93.3%
Count	49	38	25	15
Nations with a prob of .75 or higher				
Probability	66.7%	91.7%	88.9%	100.0%
Count	18	12	9	4

Likewise, the nations with a higher probability (.75 and higher) follow the expected mathematical likelihood closely; 12 out of 18 (66.7%) entered into a violent conflict the next year, 11 out of 12 (91.7%) entered into a violent conflict within 2 years, 8 out of 9 (88.9%) within 3 years and four out of four (100%) entered into a violent conflict within four years. The data is implying that nations the model incorrectly predicts to be in a violent conflict have all of the factors necessary for violent conflict and have a high probability of entering into a violent conflict in the near future.

These actual predictions and results follow closely to the mathematical likelihood. A nation with a probability of 0.5 of being in a violent conflict would have a 0.75 probability of being in a violent conflict the following year (assumes the conditions do not change). Comparing Table 22 and Table 21, it is evident that the actual data behaves reasonably as mathematically expected. Note that these mathematical likelihoods are strictly for 0.5 and 0.75 while the actual results are of nations with a 0.5 and higher and with a 0.75 and higher. Nonetheless, the results can be used to assign risk value to a nation entering violent conflict in the near future.

Forecasting the Future: 2014

Trial Model 14 is applied to the 2014 data and the predictions are shown in Figure 39. The model predicts 71 nations in a violent conflict and an additional 12 nations in a violent conflict when the cut off value is adjusted to .28. Sixty eight of the 83 violent conflict nations were previously in conflict in 2013 and 15 of the nations (outlined in a bold box) are new to violent conflict. According to the historical percentages previously discussed, any false predictions in the red box in Figure 39 have greater than 66% likelihood of entering into a violent conflict the next year and almost a near certainty of entering into a violent conflict within 2-4 years.

2014 Predictions

Year	Nation	Group	Probability
2014	Greece	OECD	1.00
2014	Mexico	OECD	1.00
2014	Turkey	OECD	1.00
2014	Nicaragua	Latin America	1.00
2014	Yemen	Arab	1.00
2014	Bangladesh	S and E Asia	1.00
2014	Haiti	Latin America	1.00
2014	Egypt	Arab	1.00
2014	Indonesia	S and E Asia	0.99
2014	Lao People's Democratic Republic	S and E Asia	0.99
2014	Cambodia	S and E Asia	0.98
2014	Democratic Republic of the Congo	Sub Sahara	0.98
2014	Comoros	Sub Sahara	0.97
2014	Iraq	Arab	0.97
2014	Chile	OECD	0.97
2014	Honduras	Latin America	0.96
2014	Philippines	S and E Asia	0.96
2014	Pakistan	E Europe C Asia	0.96
2014	Somalia	Sub Sahara	0.95
2014	Mali	Sub Sahara	0.94
2014	Cameroon	Sub Sahara	0.92
2014	Colombia	Latin America	0.92
2014	Swaziland	Sub Sahara	0.91
2014	Russian Federation	E Europe C Asia	0.90
2014	Guatemala	Latin America	0.90
2014	Paraguay	Latin America	0.90
2014	Rwanda	Sub Sahara	0.89
2014	Algeria	Arab	0.88
2014	Ethiopia	Sub Sahara	0.88
2014	Armenia	E Europe C Asia	0.87
2014	Central African Republic	Sub Sahara	0.87
2014	Lebanon	Arab	0.86
2014	Nigeria	Sub Sahara	0.86
2014	Afghanistan	E Europe C Asia	0.86
2014	Nepal	S and E Asia	0.86
2014	China	S and E Asia	0.85
2014	Guinea	Sub Sahara	0.85
2014	Bahrain	Arab	0.84
2014	Angola	Sub Sahara	0.84
2014	India	S and E Asia	0.83
2014	Morocco	Arab	0.82
2014	Kazakhstan	E Europe C Asia	0.82
2014	Sudan	Sub Sahara	0.82
2014	France	OECD	0.81
2014	Peru	Latin America	0.80
2014	Azerbaijan	E Europe C Asia	0.80
2014	Venezuela	Latin America	0.79
2014	Myanmar	S and E Asia	0.79
2014	Thailand	S and E Asia	0.78
2014	Democratic People's Republic of Korea	S and E Asia	0.76
2014	Guinea Bissau	Sub Sahara	0.75

Nations that the Model predicts are in conflict with a probability of .75 or higher

Year	Nation	Group	Probability
2014	Saudi Arabia	Arab	0.74
2014	United Republic of Tanzania	Sub Sahara	0.70
2014	Tajikistan	E Europe C Asia	0.68
2014	Iran (Islamic Republic of)	E Europe C Asia	0.65
2014	Sri Lanka	S and E Asia	0.62
2014	Ecuador	Latin America	0.61
2014	Oman	Arab	0.60
2014	United Arab Emirates	Arab	0.59
2014	Jordan	Arab	0.58
2014	Zimbabwe	Sub Sahara	0.57
2014	South Sudan	Sub Sahara	0.56
2014	South Africa	Sub Sahara	0.56
2014	Chad	Sub Sahara	0.56
2014	Kuwait	Arab	0.56
2014	Malawi	Sub Sahara	0.56
2014	Bolivia	Latin America	0.55
2014	Gabon	Sub Sahara	0.52
2014	Viet Nam	S and E Asia	0.52
2014	Zambia	Sub Sahara	0.51
2014	Bosnia and Herzegovina	E Europe C Asia	0.50

Nations that the Model predicts are in conflict with a probabiltiy between .5 and .75

Year	Nation	Group	Probability
2014	Kyrgyzstan	E Europe C Asia	0.50
2014	Ukraine	E Europe C Asia	0.47
2014	Albania	E Europe C Asia	0.47
2014	Georgia	E Europe C Asia	0.47
2014	Israel	OECD	0.46
2014	Uzbekistan	E Europe C Asia	0.42
2014	Tunisia	Arab	0.40
2014	Syrian Arab Republic	Arab	0.40
2014	Sierra Leone	Sub Sahara	0.37
2014	Papua New Guinea	S and E Asia	0.37
2014	Uganda	Sub Sahara	0.36
2014	Burundi	Sub Sahara	0.33

Nations that the Model predicts are in conflict when the cutoff is adjusted to .28

Nations new to conflict have a black box around them

Figure 39: 2014 Predictions

Forecasting the Future: 2015

Trial Model 14 is then applied to the 2015 data and the predictions are shown in Figure 40. The model predicts 72 nations in a violent conflict and an additional 13 nations in a violent conflict when the cut off value is adjusted to .28. Sixty eight of the 85 violent conflict nations were previously in violent conflict in 2013. Seventeen nations are new to conflict since the 2013 HIIK report, 11 of them were also predicted in 2014 (light blue) and 6 of the nations (outlined in a bold box) are new to violent conflict since 2014.

2015 Predictions

Year	Nation	Group	Probability
2015	Greece	OECD	1.00
2015	Mexico	OECD	1.00
2015	Republic of Korea	OECD	1.00
2015	Turkey	OECD	1.00
2015	Nicaragua	Latin America	1.00
2015	Yemen	Arab	1.00
2015	Bangladesh	S and E Asia	1.00
2015	Haiti	Latin America	1.00
2015	Central African Republic	Sub Sahara	1.00
2015	Egypt	Arab	1.00
2015	Hungary	OECD	1.00
2015	Cambodia	S and E Asia	0.99
2015	Swaziland	Sub Sahara	0.99
2015	Indonesia	S and E Asia	0.99
2015	Lao People's Democratic Republic	S and E Asia	0.98
2015	Democratic Republic of the Congo	Sub Sahara	0.98
2015	Venezuela	Latin America	0.98
2015	Honduras	Latin America	0.97
2015	Philippines	S and E Asia	0.96
2015	Lebanon	Arab	0.96
2015	Chile	OECD	0.96
2015	Pakistan	E Europe C Asia	0.96
2015	Iraq	Arab	0.93
2015	Cameroon	Sub Sahara	0.92
2015	Comoros	Sub Sahara	0.91
2015	Russian Federation	E Europe C Asia	0.90
2015	Guatemala	Latin America	0.90
2015	Colombia	Latin America	0.90
2015	Angola	Sub Sahara	0.89
2015	Algeria	Arab	0.89
2015	Afghanistan	E Europe C Asia	0.88
2015	Zimbabwe	Sub Sahara	0.87
2015	China	S and E Asia	0.87
2015	Nigeria	Sub Sahara	0.87
2015	Armenia	E Europe C Asia	0.86
2015	Paraguay	Latin America	0.86
2015	Nepal	S and E Asia	0.84
2015	Ecuador	Latin America	0.83
2015	Ethiopia	Sub Sahara	0.83
2015	Morocco	Arab	0.83
2015	India	S and E Asia	0.83
2015	Bahrain	Arab	0.82
2015	France	OECD	0.82
2015	Myanmar	S and E Asia	0.82
2015	Kazakhstan	E Europe C Asia	0.81
2015	Thailand	S and E Asia	0.79
2015	United Republic of Tanzania	Sub Sahara	0.78
2015	Guinea Bissau	Sub Sahara	0.78
2015	Peru	Latin America	0.78
2015	Sudan	Sub Sahara	0.78
2015	Democratic People's Republic of Korea	S and E Asia	0.76

Nations that the Model predicts are in conflict with a probability of .75 or higher

Year	Nation	Group	Probability
2015	Rwanda	Sub Sahara	0.74
2015	South Sudan	Sub Sahara	0.73
2015	Saudi Arabia	Arab	0.72
2015	Azerbaijan	E Europe C Asia	0.72
2015	Chad	Sub Sahara	0.71
2015	Guinea	Sub Sahara	0.71
2015	Iran (Islamic Republic of)	E Europe C Asia	0.66
2015	United Arab Emirates	Arab	0.66
2015	Tajikistan	E Europe C Asia	0.65
2015	Sri Lanka	S and E Asia	0.63
2015	Jordan	Arab	0.61
2015	Somalia	Sub Sahara	0.60
2015	Niger	Sub Sahara	0.59
2015	Oman	Arab	0.58
2015	Viet Nam	S and E Asia	0.58
2015	South Africa	Sub Sahara	0.55
2015	Kuwait	Arab	0.52
2015	Albania	E Europe C Asia	0.51
2015	Ukraine	E Europe C Asia	0.51
2015	Bosnia and Herzegovina	E Europe C Asia	0.50
2015	Bolivia	Latin America	0.50

Nations that the Model predicts are in conflict with a probabiltiy between .5 and .75

Year	Nation	Group	Probability
2015	Mali	Sub Sahara	0.49
2015	Syrian Arab Republic	Arab	0.48
2015	Gabon	Sub Sahara	0.47
2015	Uzbekistan	E Europe C Asia	0.46
2015	Zambia	Sub Sahara	0.46
2015	Dominican Republic	Latin America	0.44
2015	Georgia	E Europe C Asia	0.43
2015	Kyrgyzstan	E Europe C Asia	0.42
2015	Sierra Leone	Sub Sahara	0.41
2015	Uganda	Sub Sahara	0.38
2015	Tunisia	Arab	0.37
2015	Papua New Guinea	S and E Asia	0.32
2015	Burundi	Sub Sahara	0.31

Nations that the Model predicts are in conflict when the cutoff is adjusted to .28

Nations new to conflict have a black box around them

Nations new to conflict since 2013 (last HIIK report) but also predicted in 2014

Figure 40: 2015 Predictions

Note the Republic of Korea (South Korea) near the top of the 2015 prediction list. This is not an anomaly or errant prediction, this nation was in a state of violent conflict in 2009 and in 2010 and the model correctly predicted both years with the same probability

93

that it predicts in 2015. Looking at the model variables in 2009 and 2010, the model predicted South Korea to have a violent conflict because of its sharp decrease in trade, rise in infant mortality and lower than average caloric intake (relative to South Korea in previous years). In 2015 the prediction of violence is attributed to the increase in the "Freedom" score (lower is better); meaning political oppression increased in South Korea and the model predicts violence in 2015.

Investigative Questions Answered

How accurately can a Logistic Regression Model predict the state of the world; nations that will be in a state of "violent conflict" and nations that will not?

A one world model can predict the state of the world with almost 75% accuracy. Six sub-models can predict the state of the world with greater than 78% accuracy and greater than 80% accuracy when cut off parameters are adjusted to 0.28.

What are the key variables that contribute to a nation being in a state of violent conflict?

The one world model uses 15 variables, including 14 main effects and one 2nd order polynomial. The five most significant of these factors are "Freedom", "Region", "Trade", "Improved Water" and "Polity IV". The six sub-models differ in variable size from three to ten. The significant variables vary but "Freedom" remains the most significant variable for Sub Sahara Africa, Eastern Europe & Central Asia and OECD. "Death rate" is the most important variable for Arab and Latin American nations and caloric intake is the most important variable for South and East Asian nations. "Freedom" and "Trade" are present in five out of six sub-models.

Given a nation is falsely predicted to be in a violent conflict, how likely is it to enter into a violent conflict the following year or within 2-4 years?

Nations the model falsely predicts to be in a violent conflict have all the factors necessary for violent conflict. According to the historical predictions and accuracies, a nation incorrectly predicted to be in a violent conflict (with a probability of .5 or higher) but is actually not in violent conflict has a 59 % chance of entering into a violent conflict the following year, a 79% chance of entering a violent conflict within the next two years, a 88% of entering a violent conflict within the next 3 years and a 93% chance of entering a violent conflict within the next 4 years.

A nation incorrectly predicted to be in a violent conflict (with a probability of .75 or higher) but is actually not in violent conflict has a 67% chance of entering into a violent conflict the following year, a 92% chance of entering a violent conflict within the next two years, a 89% of entering a violent conflict within the next 3 years and a 100% chance of entering a violent conflict within the next 4 years. The historical data indicates that the expected mathematical likelihoods can be applied to future years.

Summary

This chapter constructed and provided analysis for 14 trial models, creating a "best whole world" model and a "best overall model" which consisted of six sub-models. Dominant variables were identified, sensitivity analysis showed the robustness of the model and predictions were made for 2014 and 2015. Additional analysis concerning the false predictions provided answers to two of the study questions.

V. Conclusions and Recommendations

Conclusions of Research

This study analyzed 27 variables to predict the future state of the world where nations will either be in a state of "violent conflict" or "not in violent conflict". A whole world logistic regression model can predict violent conflict with 75% accuracy while six sub-models can accurately predict violent conflict with over 80% accuracy. The accuracy of the final model is among the best found in literature. A nations "Freedom" score, which is an average of civil liberties and political rights, is the dominant global factor for violent conflict. What region a nation is in and how much they trade are other significant factors of violent conflict. The significant variables differ from region to region.

Significance of Research

This study can assist decisions makers in planning for predicted violent conflict in nations throughout the world. The study can also help decision makers identify factors that lead to violent conflict in an effort to improve these factor areas before violence occurs.

Recommendations for Action

The six sub-models can be applied to future years to predict violent conflict in the world. The significant variables identified in this study can be useful for future model builders and for decision makers attempting to increase stability in nations. The whole world model can also be used as a template for future world models.

Recommendations for Future Research

Three of the variables were locked and did not change from year to year. Yearly data for "Regime type" Ethnic diversity" and "Religious diversity" would offer a more dynamic model. Regime type" and "Religious diversity" especially have the potential to impact the model and be valuable predictors. The six sub-models proved the best predictors of violence. Future studies could focus on one region at a time and build a better model for that specific region. Subject matter experts can advise new variables for each region as new data becomes available and different cut offs for each sub-model might also yield better results. A variable that will account for nations in a violent conflict outside of its borders could prove significant and reduce noise introduced by stable nations entering into conflict by choice.

The study was limited by availability of the dependent variable. The Heidelberg Institute for Conflict Research was updating their database and was unable to provide data for this study. The data was collected through AFIT analysts parsing through difficult pdf documents. Future research would benefit from a larger database than the 2008-2013 database that was used for this study.

Appendix A: List of nations in each region

Sub Saharan Africa - 49 Nations
Angola
Benin
Botswana
Burkina Faso
Burundi
Cabo Verde
Cameroon
Central African Republic
Chad
Comoros
Congo
Côte D'Ivoire
Democratic Republic of the Congo
Djibouti
Equatorial Guinea
Eritrea
Ethiopia
Gabon
Gambia
Ghana
Guinea
Guinea Bissau
Kenya
Lesotho
Liberia
Madagascar
Malawi
Mali
Mauritania
Mauritius
Mozambique
Namibia
Niger
Nigeria
Rwanda
Sao Tome and Principe
Senegal
Seychelles
Sierra Leone
Somalia
South Africa
South Sudan
Sudan
Swaziland
Togo
Uganda
United Republic of Tanzania
Zambia
Zimbabwe
Grand Total

Arab - 17 Nations
Algeria
Bahrain
Egypt
Iraq
Jordan
Kuwait
Lebanon
Libya
Morocco
Oman
Qatar
Saudi Arabia
Syrian Arab Republic
Tunisia
United Arab Emirates
West Bank and Gaza
Yemen

South & East Asia - 28 Nations
Bangladesh
Bhutan
Brunei Darussalam
Cambodia
China
Democratic People's Republic of Korea
Fiji
India
Indonesia
Kiribati
Lao People s Democratic Republic
Malaysia
Maldives
Micronesia (Federated States of)
Mongolia
Myanmar
Nepal
Papua New Guinea
Philippines
Samoa
Singapore
Solomon Islands
Sri Lanka
Thailand
Timor-Leste
Tonga
Vanuatu
Viet Nam

OECD - 33 Nations
Australia
Austria
Belgium
Canada
Chile
Czech Republic
Denmark
Estonia
Finland
France
Germany
Greece
Hungary
Iceland
Ireland
Israel
Italy
Japan
Luxembourg
Mexico
Netherlands
New Zealand
Norway
Poland
Portugal
Republic of Korea
Slovenia
Spain
Sweden
Switzerland
Turkey
United Kingdom of Great Britain and Northern Ireland
United States of America

East Europe& Central Asia - 28 Nations
Afghanistan
Albania
Armenia
Azerbaijan
Belarus
Bosnia and Herzegovina
Bulgaria
Croatia
Cyprus
Georgia
Iran (Islamic Republic of)
Kazakhstan
Kyrgyzstan
Latvia
Lithuania
Malta
Montenegro
Pakistan
Republic of Moldova
Romania
Russian Federation
Serbia
Slovakia
Tajikistan
The former Yugoslav Republic of Macedonia
Turkmenistan
Ukraine
Uzbekistan

Latin America - 27 Nations
Antigua and Barbuda
Argentina
Bahamas
Barbados
Belize
Bolivia
Brazil
Colombia
Costa Rica
Cuba
Dominican Republic
Ecuador
El Salvador
Grenada
Guatemala
Guyana
Haiti
Honduras
Jamaica
Nicaragua
Panama
Paraguay
Peru
Suriname
Trinidad and Tobago
Uruguay
Venezuela
Grand Total

Bibliography

Allison, P. (2013, March 5). *Why I Don't Trust the Hosmer-Lemeshow Test for Logistic Regression*. Retrieved February 27, 2015, from Statistical Horizons: http://www.statisticalhorizons.com/hosmer-lemeshow

Bigley, A. L. (2013). *Horn's Curve Estimation Through Multi-Dimensional Interpolation*. Wright-Patterson AFB, OH: Air Force Institute of Technology MS Thesis.

Box, G. E. (1979). *Robustness in the strategy of scientific model building*. New York City: Academic Press.

Center for Systemic Peace. (2014). *Integrated Netrwork for Societal Conflict Research Data Page*. Retrieved November 3, 2014, from Center for Systemic Peace: http://www.systemicpeace.org/inscrdata.html

Christakis, N. A. (2012, April 18). *The World's 100 Most Influential People: 2012*. Retrieved February 26, 2015, from TIME: http://content.time.com/time/specials/packages/article/0,28804,2111975_2111976_2112170,00.html

Food and Agriculture Organization of the United Nations. (2014). *Databases*. Retrieved October 24, 2014, from Food and Agriculture Organization of the United Nations: http://www.fao.org/statistics/databases/en/

Freedom House. (2012). *Methodology`*. Retrieved 11 3, 2014, from Freedom House: http://www.freedomhouse.org/report-types/freedom-world

Gapminder, A fact-based worldview. (n.d.). Retrieved from http://www.gapminder.org/

Goldstone, J. A. (2005). *A global forecasting model of political instability. Political Instability Task Force*.

Heidelberg Institute for International Conflict Research. (2014). *Conflict Barometer 2013*. Heidelberg: Heidleberg Institute for Conflict Research.

Hinrichs, C. a. (2010). *JMP Essentials: An Illustrated Step-byStep Guide for New users.* . Cary, North Carolina: SAS Institute Inc.

Horn, J. L. (1965). A Rationale and Test for the number of Factors in Factor Analysis. *Pscychometrika* , 179-185.

King, M. (2014). *Optimizing Counterinsurgency Operations, Dissertation submitted to the Faculty and the Board of Trustees of the Colorado School of Mines 90.7.* Colorado School of Mines.

Linear V. Logistic Regression. (n.d.). Retrieved 09 13, 2014, from http://www.janda.org/workshop/Discriminant%20analysis/Talk/talk01.htm

Menard, S. (2001). *Applied Logistic Regression Analysis, 2nd Editions.* Thousand Oaks, California: Sage University Papers Series on Quantitative Applicatiosn in the Social Sciences, 07-106.

Montomgery, D. (2012). *Introduction to Linear Regression Analysis.* Hoboken, New Jersey: John Wiley & Sons, Inc.

SAS Institute. (2015). *Multivariate platform options.* Retrieved 2015, from jmp. Statistcal Discovery from SAS: http://www.jmp.com/support/help/Multivariate_Platform_Options.shtml#106307

Shearer, R. (2010). Recognizing Patterns of Nation-State Instability that Lead to Conflict. *Military Operations Research 15.3* , 17-29.

The best stats you've ever seen. (2006). Retrieved January 2015, from Ted Talks: http://www.ted.com/talks/hans_rosling_shows_the_best_stats_you_ve_ever_seen

The Fund for Peace . (2015). *FFP.* Retrieved 2014, from Fragile States Index: http://ffp.statesindex.org/

The Geometer's Sketchpad Resource Center. (2014). *The Geometer's Sketchpad Resource Center.* Retrieved October 6, 2014, from Least Squares: http://www.dynamicgeometry.com/General_Resources/Advanced_Sketch_Gallery/Other_Explorations/Statistics_Collection/Least_Squares.html

United Nations. (2013). *Supply, Crops, Primary Equivalent (FAOSTAT) Dataset.* Retrieved 2014, from Food and Agriculture Organization of the United Nations: http://data.fao.org/dataset-data-filter?entryId=c0643f7c-9bf6-43f4-a2bb-fae4e50f4c2e&tab=data&type=Measure&uuidResource=c2abbcfe-e37c-42b9-a90a-9bbe2b86701f

World Bank. (2015). *Data.* Retrieved 2014, from The World Bank: http://data.worldbank.org/

www.ingramcontent.com/pod-product-compliance
Lightning Source LLC
Chambersburg PA
CBHW081225280526
45787CB00006B/2531